READY, AIM, HIRED
DEVELOPING YOUR
BRAND NAME RESUME

READY, AIM, HIRED
DEVELOPING YOUR
BRAND NAME RESUME

Allan Karson
President of Allan Karson Associates Inc.
An Executive Search Firm

BUSINESS ONE IRWIN
Homewood, Illinois 60430

© RICHARD D. IRWIN, INC., 1991

Senior editor: Jeffrey A. Krames
Project editor: Margaret A. Schmidt
Production manager: Ann Cassady
Cover designer: Renée Klyczek-Nordstrom
Compositor: TCSystems, Inc.
Typeface: 11/13 Century Schoolbook
Printer: Malloy Lithographing, Inc.

Library of Congress Cataloging-in-Publication Data

Karson, Allan.
    Ready, aim, hired: developing your brand name résumé / by Allan Karson.
      p.   cm.
    ISBN 1-55623-368-X
     1. Résumés (Employment) 2. Job hunting.   I. Title
    HF5383.K38 1991
     650.14—dc20   90–3064
                                                    CIP

Printed in the United States of America

1 2 3 4 5 6 7 8 9 0 ML 7 6 5 4 3 2 1 0

This book is dedicated to all the people who have ever looked for a job in the labyrinth that is called the U.S. job market. And it is also dedicated to their wives or husbands; their boyfriends or girlfriends; and their parents, who gave them moral and, sometimes, financial support in what is a very difficult individual endeavor—and to the children, who have the trying, helpless experience of watching a parent look for a job.

PREFACE

I run my own executive search firm. An executive search firm receives search assignments from corporations to recruit executives for positions in the client firm. The term sometimes applied to this profession is *headhunting*. Prior to starting my search firm, I was a line manager in industry for more than 25 years.

My search firm concentrates on serving firms whose products and services are based on high technology products. These firms are primarily in the computer, telecommunications, data communication, and electronic industries. Most of the positions I seek to fill are at the level of director, vice president, and president and chief executive officer (CEO). I specialize in technical, marketing, and general management positions.

All day long, I have telephone conversations with people at all levels in firms—people who are candidates for a position, people who are references for candidates, people whom I ask to refer me to potential candidates. At least once each week, I meet face-to-face with people who are being evaluated for a specific job or who are considering looking for a job. Also I review a sizable quantity of résumés that are sent to me daily from people in varied industrial and service sectors such as banking, construction, heavy manufacturing, and high technology. My activities always have something to do with evaluating a person for a job.

Many people call me when they are looking for advice on the general status of industry, on the vigor of the job market, on whether they should be looking for a job—as well as how they should be looking. They call me because I have insight into the high technology industry and what it takes to get a job.

In addition, I am interested in people, and I am willing to spend time with them. I am an empathetic, good listener. In particular, for people forced to look for a job, I realize in my gut what they may be going through and what their problems are. I therefore try to help them as much as I can. A form of public service, you might say, but the topic is always centered on the issue of how to evaluate a person for a job.[1]

Many of these people send their résumés to me. They may call me in a few days to see how I evaluated their résumé and whether I know of a position that may be open and is appropriate to their background. I cover both issues during that subsequent call. That is one way that I get to see résumés—but it is not the main way. The main way is through the few hundred unsolicited résumés that are sent to my firm each week by people who know of my firm's specialty or résumés sent in response to an advertisement we may have placed in a newspaper or those sent by many outplacement firms who have the firm on their mailing lists—myriads of résumés.

We pore over these résumés for two types of job candidates: (1) people who

---

[1] People look for a job, a source of income, or work. These terms, for the most part, are equivalent when we talk about the job market. When a person says he is looking for a *position,* he is looking for a job. A position is a *location* in an organization. Thus, we will use the word *job* in this book.

are directly applicable to positions we are presently seeking to fill and (2) people with a strong background who may be applicable to a search we may undertake in the future. We are dead earnest in trying to identify the best. We work at it—for ourselves and for the candidate—to make sure that we did not neglect something in the résumé that it is directly applicable to our searches or otherwise distinguishes the candidate.

But our task is made difficult by the fact that people's written presentations—their résumé and cover letter—do not do justice to themselves. In all but a rare few, no matter what their experience and business level may be—the first line supervisor, the sales manager, the chief operating officer (COO), and even the chief executive officer (CEO)—*they do not present themselves to the reader in such a way that the reader would be attracted to them.*

They have a minimal understanding of what it takes to make a person want to read and appreciate a cover letter and a résumé—and be sufficiently interested to make the effort to call them in to be presented to a prospective employer. They do not know how to sell themselves in the job market.

I believe most corporate managers of human resources, as well as recruiters and members of executive search firms, can make a similar observation. It is true they sometimes receive good—and, now and then, excellent—résumés and cover letters. But these are rare, no more than 5 percent of the total.

I suppose that most of these job seekers have read one or two books that advise people how to write a cover letter and résumé. While those books may have been applicable in the past, *I believe that the design for résumés advocated in the books found on the shelves of bookstores has not kept up with the present job market—nor with today's business environment.* This book seeks to remedy that situation by presenting a new approach, the *brand name* résumé.

ACKNOWLEDGMENTS

I wish to thank the many people who have presented their résumés to me and graciously received my comments about how they should change their résumés according to my *brand name* techniques.

I would also like to thank people who reviewed an early manuscript and provided advice and comments about the structure and contents of this book and the need for such a new approach—friends such as Dave Caplan and Dr. Howard Frank and my brother Marvin, who suggested the inclusion of "before" and "after" résumés to show the value of the brand name concept.

Finally, I thank our son Michael, who typed the original draft; Philip Koslow, who edited the original manuscript; Steve Holly, who was always ready to help me when I ran into any hardware or software problems on my MAC; Vicki Toffler, who helped me complete the final manuscript and prepared with me the "before" and "after" résumés, providing her solid criticism; and my wife Inge, who gave me "space" to write this book.

Allan Karson

CONTENTS

PART IV
PERSONAL PROFILES—COVER LETTERS
AND RESUMES

PART V
SETS OF COVER LETTERS AND RESUMES

PART VI
LOOKING FOR A JOB WITH YOUR BRAND
NAME RESUME—General Advice and Thoughts about the Job
Search

PART VII
MY FINAL REMARKS—SOME HOMILIES

LIST OF RESUMES

ABOUT THIS BOOK

This book is written for professionals—people who seek management or specialized positions or people with college degrees. They may have had a long and successful job history, or they may be recent college graduates. For all people, there is a common denominator in job seeking—to get an interview with the potential employer. This book will tell you how to prepare the key ingredients needed to attain that goal—a meaningful cover letter and résumé.

This book is based on hundreds of contacts with people in the job market who asked me to review their letters and résumés to help improve them. And just as important, it is based on the observed "flatness" or "grayness" of the thousands of résumés that I have reviewed during my professional career—résumés that lacked vigor, individuality, and verve.

> Saying that you are "a dynamic, creative, successful, bottom-line oriented, market-sensitive, team builder (etc., etc.) executive" does not establish your brand. It just puts you in a pile with thousands of other job seekers. It means nothing but *words, words, words. Show me!*

This book equips you with a specific road map of do's and don'ts about writing résumés. Along with the good features to present in your résumé, it gives examples of what I consider to be poor ways to present yourself in a résumé—ways that tend to give the reader a negative impression of you. Unless you have the *correct* ways to write about yourself in your job-search, it is as if you were going on a trip in your car without gas. I will give you the gas (high-test) to get you started and to keep it going. Where you go, how you go, and how fast you go are your decisions.

To show clearly what we consider to be a weak and a strong résumé, this book presents ficticious résumés that incorporate features that are found in most résumés. These résumés are annotated to point out the weak and strong features. Many of the résumés are revised according to the principles of this book, resulting in stronger résumés: "before" and "after" presentations. You will be able to see the differences, and you will be able to be the judge of what constitutes a good résumé.

The book also presents the rationale for a strong, brand name résumé. It has charts that you will use to define your résumé. The book describes how these charts can be used to help you resolve that key issue, *where* to look for a job.

In addition to suggestions about the résumé, the book contains many specific things you should do in your search—the nitty-gritty of how to set up your home so that you conduct your search in a professional way—the message to put on your answering machine, the proper speaker of that message, the consideration of an additional phone line at home, and so forth.

I suggest you read other books on the subject of how to look for a job. You will see that they present background and information on the job market in general—what I call the "job-seeking industry"—which may or may not be useful to you. You will also observe that most of them are much longer than this book. The subjects usually described in these books are how to network among your friends and business colleagues, how to find where a position is open, the role of search firms and recruiters, how to prepare for an interview, what to wear and what to say at an interview, placing and replying to ads in newspapers, following up on calls, and so on—the scenery of the trip. They usually present a chapter on the résumé, but appear to consider it a side issue in the job search. It is not.[2]

We will not talk about scenery. We will talk about getting from where you are to where you want to be. You can choose your own destination, your own timing, your own style, your own media to get your message across. This book tells you what to include in your message. It is *what* you need to get *you* your job.

---

[2] While I was preparing this book, I made an analysis of the various how-to-get-a-job books in bookstores. I saw that they were wordy and were not truly directed at helping someone who had an immediate problem. They were more of a course on job seeking than a help in preparing for a key exam—as if your car broke down and you asked for help, you were given a 300-page service manual on your car, or if you were drowning and yelled for a lifeline, someone threw you a book on swimming.

PART I

THE OVERALL PLAN

SECTION 1: The Critical Importance of Your Résumé

There are two ways to get a job: (1) you know the employer, and he hires you without asking for any written information about you or (2) as is the case with most of us, you submit a résumé to represent you. And you hope that your cover letter and résumé are so interesting, positive, and attractive—just what the reader is looking for—that the employer will contact you for an interview. That is what the cover letter and résumé are for—to get the reader to contact you. That is all. Their use is not to get the job, not to negotiate a salary, not to tell your complete life history—just to get that initial contact.

Résumés, therefore, play a key role in the vast majority of hirings. They are needed when you want to meet a human resource manager, answer an ad in a newspaper, or send an unsolicited letter to a prospective employer. The résumé is the most important means you have to present yourself. It is probably the only way that you have to present yourself.

Many writers who have prepared advisory books on how to get a job speak disparagingly of résumés. They say that résumés are not that important, claiming that very few jobs are gotten through résumés, in comparison with the number of résumés that are mailed out. And they also say that human resource people do not truly read the résumé. I disagree with them. My rebuttal is this: If résumés are often ineffective or ignored, it is because those résumés are misdirected or poorly constructed.

For example, I observe individuals and outplacement firms sending résumés helter-skelter in response to newspaper ads, with the person's background not being anything like the requirements stated in the ad. And I receive résumés describing people who are in a profession or functional area that is distinctly different from my firm's advertised specialty. Sending a poor résumé (or even a good one) describing your background as a director of marketing in response to an ad looking for a general manager is probably a waste of time and effort and should not be, in any way, considered a reflection of the value of résumés.

Also, most résumés are boring to read, and most résumés do not properly represent the person. They do not distinguish the person from thousands of competitors in the job market. They do not describe the uniqueness of the individual. The job-seeker should, therefore, prepare an excellent selling résumé and send it selectively to places where there is a good chance of success. Remember, the résumé is probably the only way that you have to present yourself.

1

Résumés are being written today as they were 30 years ago. While there may be some improvements in the recommended format, such as where the job-seeker is advised to describe accomplishments in addition to providing a chronologically organized description of jobs and education, these are not enough. A much stronger editorial guidance for content and presentation is required.

What is needed is what we will call a "brand name" presentation. This is more than a way of presenting your qualifications. Its purpose is to make you *stand out* against the competition. Remember—you are not the only person seeking that job. You are competing with others. You need to establish *your* brand name. Exxon, Sony, Canon, GM, Xerox, Procter and Gamble, Lever Brothers, and thousands of successful firms recognized long ago the need to distinguish themselves, and they made it an essential part of their sales campaign. You too, must establish *your* brand name.[3]

When you use the brand name technique, you will continue to present your personal, education, and career history, but you will first identify features that make you outstanding and that differentiate you from others. You will concentrate on these features and build your résumé around them. You will also organize your résumé so that the reader will quickly and easily see your brand name features.

Your résumé will emphasize the features that are most meaningful to your reader. And just as importantly, it will reduce or do away with the irrelevancies. You have but *one or two pages* with which to present yourself. You have but *a few moments of the reader's time* to make sure the right impression of you gets across. Use your space and time carefully. A brand name approach is designed to get *your* message across.

SECTION 2:   Starting Out

Since people think of looking for a new job under a wide variety of circumstances, this book applies to all. You will need a cover letter and résumé—no matter what the circumstances are.

- You have just graduated from college with a bachelor's degree, a master's, or a Ph.D.
- You are presently employed but are considering leaving because your firm is relocating, and while you want to stay with the firm, you do not want to make the relocation.
- You feel uncomfortable with your present boss.

---

[3] What is a brand name? People like to identify with well-known names. They often buy a car because they associate the name with luxury or performance, buy clothes because of the label, and send their children to schools with prestigious names. When they tell friends they have dined out or gone on vacation, they are sure to emphasize the name of the restaurant and the name of the hotel where they stayed. They seek to have the listener recognize and appreciate the names they are associated with and to receive the respect that goes along with the product or establishment. Thus, the brand name identifies the product, and the user receives some of the product's reflected glory. It is used by individuals to promote their "standing" in the social community. A brand name is part of the fabric of everyone's personal and business life. It is a technique that can be used by a job-seeker to promote himself or herself in the business community.

- There is a leveraged buyout (LBO) or a takeover by another firm, and you're not sure where you are going to end up.
- You feel that there is not enough opportunity for advancement for you in this firm.
- Family circumstances require you to return to or leave your hometown.
- You are not sufficiently recognized for your value.
- You just got a lateral promotion, and you feel you should rise in the organization.
- The firm has grown to a large size, and the relaxed, friendly, and convivial atmosphere is gone.
- You are underutilized and bored.
- You want to move to "get away from it all."
- The firm is installing a mandatory early retirement program, and you are not ready to stop working.
- You have just been fired.

People in any of these situations come to me and ask how to go about looking for a job. I indicate they should prepare a résumé as soon as possible so that I can understand what they have to offer and evaluate how well they present themselves. A résumé can also tell an experienced reader of résumés what you think of yourself and how you view your position in industry—a key factor in how you are evaluated by human resource people.

Some people say to me, when I advise them to prepare a résumé as soon as they can, "I am too busy right now." I don't understand this. *A résumé is not something to be done in your spare time. It is something to be worked on intensely and as soon as possible. No one who wants a job can lack the time to prepare a résumé and to keep it updated.* If your boss said that you should prepare a vital document—and the résumé is the vital document in any job search—I am certain that you would do it that very day and sacrifice an evening or a weekend if necessary.

The hardest part of getting a solid job campaign underway is just making the first effort and working at it. As I was once told by a famous novelist when I asked him how he goes about starting and writing a book, "It requires discipline—daily discipline. No one is waiting for my book." Similarly, no one is waiting for you. You have to make it happen. But before you go off and start calling people and sending mailers, consider what this process consists of.

Looking for a job is similar to developing and selling a product. Product people (e.g., Lever Brothers, Xerox, Canon, IBM, Pillsbury, Nabisco, Ford) know how to do this. They spend a lot of time defining what the product is, defining the channels of distribution for selling it, and preparing sales literature. Only after all that is done do they actually go out to introduce and sell the product in stores, at shows, by telephone calls, newspaper ads, TV commercials, product showrooms, mailings, and the like. We have something similar in the job search, and you should phase your activities in a similar way. You first define what your product truly is, handle yourself as a product, and think about similar issues. Then you prepare your sales literature—in your case, the résumé and the cover letter.

You will then define the channels through which you are going to present yourself—placing ads in a newspaper; doing a mail campaign; using your personal network of friends and business colleagues; or relying on firms specializing in outplacement, executive search or recruiting. Then there is the product introduction, consisting of getting out your mailing, making telephone calls and keeping track of them, answering ads in regional and national newspapers, and sending your résumés to various distributors (search firms, recruiters, etc.)

The last step is your selling. This is done during telephone and face-to-face meetings and interviews. A job interview can actually occur outside of the standard interview meeting held within an organizational setting. It can occur when you meet with people whom you use for referrals or when you meet people at industry shows.

For the average salaried person, the process of finding new opportunities in the United States is getting more and more difficult. Pick up any business journal—*The Wall Street Journal, Business Week, Fortune*—and see who the vast majority of corporate folk heroes are and see whether they are creators of jobs or extinguishers of jobs. I would say that they are the latter. LBOs and corporate raiders such as Boone Pickens, Asher Edelman, and Carl Icahn definitely have not been good for the job market, no matter what their public relations people say. Even in the industrial world, there are people such as Lee Iacocca (Chrysler) and Jack Welch (GE) who are deified by the business community and the business press for cutting back jobs. Therefore, you have a tough road, and you have to concentrate very thoughtfully on this total process.

SECTION 3: The Product—You

What are you? You are a "hard product," just like a tractor, a computer, a computer program, a box of cake mix, a truck, a TV or a VCR. People in the industrial world know what it takes to sell a hard product. You have to go about it just as they do. If you have a background in manufacturing, presumably you know the basic ground rules and techniques much better than most people. You probably have seen it done, and if you were in marketing and sales, you may have done it yourself.

People in the service industries (in which the product is providing a service, such as a real estate broker or a lawyer, providing a time-sharing service or a communication service, etc.) may not be that clear about how a hard product is presented. To put it simply, important features are placed up front; background information, in the back. Why? Because you must develop interest from the up-front part of the presentation, just as you make your first impression on someone in the first seconds of your meeting.

No matter what your product is, you must define it clearly, and make it memorable. You must show not so much what it can *do* for someone (as most people emphasize in a résumé) but *what it is*. Is it a space heater? Is it an automobile? Is it an elevator? Is it a motor? You have to do this with yourself so that the person to whom you're trying to sell yourself knows what is being offered. I will give examples—good and bad ones— of résumés in which there is too much ambiguity in the ways people present themselves, simply because they neglect to say *what I am.*

Your cover letter and résumé are a brochure representing a product. This brochure does not represent your aspirations, nor the firms you were associated with in the past. It represents *you.* Everything else is external to you: the jobs you did, the sales you built up, the products you've defined and created, the firms you ran. They are appendages to *you*—important ones, which should be shown off to the best advantage. Consider them as the tinsel and lights on the Christmas tree. They do the sparkling, but you are the tree.

The point of this—the need to present *you*—is that people should not have to guess what you are. People may play games in nonbusiness environments, but they do not have the time to play games in business. If a salesman has a product of lacquer-coated two-by-four beams (these are almost as good as the ubiquitous widget), he calls the purchasing agent and says, "I represent lacquer-coated two-by-four beams." He doesn't introduce himself to the purchasing agent by telling him that if the firm needs him, he has the right product, nor does he tell what the product can do. He first says, "I have lacquer-coated two-by-four beams." And then he goes on to describe the virtues, uses, and excellence of the product. You have to represent yourself the same way. Defining yourself, I believe, is the most important step in the preparation of your job search.

You must be seen in the cover letter and the résumé. If the reader of the résumé has to guess what you are, he may not bother reading your résumé. And most importantly, if you are not sure of what you are, most buyers will not talk to you. I cannot overemphasize this point—the necessity to *define what you are.*

Perhaps you are thinking that this approach is too cold-blooded. After all, we prefer to think of ourselves as *who* rather than *what.* We like to think that our inner feelings and our thoughts are at least as important as what we do in the world. All this is true, but it does not come first in the process of establishing yourself as a brand name in the job market.

It may be easier to adopt the right approach if you think of the prospective employer as a consumer besieged by appeals from thousands of merchandisers. Choices must be made, and there is only a short amount of time in which to make them. That is why brand names are so significant in retailing: they provide an immediate assurance that the buyer knows exactly what he or she is getting.

For this reason, you must give the firms you approach the opportunity to see quickly and clearly what you are. (*Who* you are as a person can be revealed in interviews or after you have been hired; it will not be revealed if your résumé is tossed aside.) You must imagine yourself, in your résumé and cover letter, placing yourself squarely in the employer's line of vision, like the Jolly Green Giant, if you will, and making a vivid and memorable impression.

Examples of what I am:

> I have had 18 years experience in the data processing industry in both sales and marketing positions, starting with IBM. I am extremely knowledgeable about mid-range computers and telecommunications products

and their application in the financial and insurance sectors. I was responsible for the introduction into these sectors of IBM's highly successful 4300 product line.

Besides my M.B.A. from Darden School of Business at the University of Virginia, I also hold a B.S. degree in Electrical Engineering from Lehigh University.

I have 10 years of product development, marketing, and sales management experience with Lever Brothers, specializing in home and maternity products. I am seeking an opportunity with a company that has a strong product development culture with sales between $50M and $500M. (Depending on the company size, the position title might include marketing manager, regional or district sales manager, product manager.)

I received an M.B.A. from the University of Colorado in 1980 and a degree in chemistry from Bucknell University in 1975.

I am 30 years of age, a graduate student of the Department of Computer Science and Engineering, North Carolina State University, Raleigh, North Carolina.

I received my B.S. degree at the Taipei Computer Institute, Taiwan, in 1982. Then I joined Computer Science for more than three years.

As a software engineer, I am good at IMB OS/MVS, DOS/VSE, UNIX operating systems and computer network. I am familiar with many kinds of programing languages: C language, Lisp, Pascal, Fortran, Prolog, Cobol, and assembly language.

I have proven my abilities in several diverse fields, such as Christmas ornaments, toys (buyer for FAO Schwartz and Nintendo), sporting goods and active wear (Spaulding Sporting Goods) and consumer packaged goods (Lever Brothers and Rubbermaid).

I am looking for a position that utilizes my background in consumer products and durables marketing, international sourcing, sales and licensing, working with outside inventors, development, licensing and vendor groups, and strategic planning.

My successful sales experience with Texas Instruments semiconductors (twice Salesman of the Year) was followed by moving to progressively more responsible positions of product management, marketing management, and business management.

Following TI, I have been making sales and marketing contributions to smaller companies such as Semi-All and Chipcom.

My capability to translate technology into customer benefits ranges from direct customer presentations to national ad campaigns. I have degrees from:

Southern Methodist University, M.B.A., Marketing and Economics, 1963

Stanford University, M.S.E.E., Digital Machine Design, 1967

University of Texas, Austin, B.S.E.E., 1961

The attached résumé describes my background in human resources (HR) management, which includes the top HR positions at Occidental Petroleum and at Dome Company of Canada.

In addition to the above, my credentials include:
- Twenty years of well-rounded HR generalist experience, including significant accomplishments in the areas of executive recruitment, training, compensation and benefits, EEO, labor relations; Human Resources Information Systems (installed same), and organizational development.
- Undergraduate degree and additional graduate work in the areas of behavioral science-industrial relations, including the University of Chicago's Manpower Planning Program.

I am currently the Sales Development Manager for Motorola's Mobile Communications Division, located in the Western Region. I've just completed a very successful year, almost doubling my region's sales from $5,000,000 to $10,000,000. I was recognized as top sales manager and won three awards last year. I have been with Motorola since 1969 and have an M.B.A. from UCLA.

I would appreciate your taking a few minutes to review my résumé. I am targeting a Fortune 500 company and specifically aiming at positions such as

Regional Sales Manager

Marketing Director

Product Manager

I am a vice president, chief financial officer (CFO), looking for a new opportunity.

As CFO of American Greetings Corporation, Inc., and as a Vice President Controller of Bemis Corporation—both leaders in the packaging and container industry—I have been the right-hand man to highly successful operational executives. I have demonstrated my capacity to combine my knowledge of business and finance to solve operational, planning and control problems. I seek a position that can lead to my being the COO.

I am currently the Director of Marketing for Nash-Finch Co., Inc., a $2.8 billion leader in the food wholesale industry. I am responsible for all aspects of marketing, strategic planning, and corporate communications—managing a $40 million operating budget and a staff of 15. I was recruited in November 1984 to Nash-Finch where I develop high-profit new products.

Prior to joining Nash-Finch, I was Group Director for Marketing and Product Development, reporting to the President of Pepsi Cola, Inc. Previously, I was a Director of Marketing at Fleming Co. and a Group Brand Manager at Provigo, Inc.

At the present time, I am Manager of Business Planning with Toyota Automobile Appliances in Lexington, Kentucky. I came to Toyota from Ford Motor Corporation, where I held managerial positions in program management and finance as well as business analysis and development. Earlier in my ten-year career, I was with Caterpillar in marketing and product management capacities. In addition, I hold a Master's Degree in Business Administration and a B.S. in Marketing and Finance from the Wharton School at the University of Pennsylvania.

I was trained at Stanford University as a research physicist, and since 1968 I have been using my technical skills in the industrial environment dealing with radiation emission. My growth has been from R&D project work to new product development management. Recently, I have been providing the technical direction and evaluating the growth opportunities for both the services and products business of Zycorp, an $80 million unit of Perkin Elmer.

A reorganization has eliminated my position, resulting in the company and me parting on good terms. I feel that my strong and uniquely diverse background, which is described in the enclosed resume, well qualifies me for a senior technical executive position in a wide variety of technology-based businesses. Some particular strengths are:

- Managing the new product development process.
- Modifying equipment to minimize radiation.
- Assessing technical products/services for business potential.

SECTION 4: Today's Business Environment

The résumés that I receive in the mail are mainly prepared according to guidelines that would have been applicable to the U.S. business environment as it existed 15 or more years ago. So much has happened in recent years to make that design obsolete. Styles change in business as in every other realm of life: Résumé styles have to change accordingly.

The following are some examples of changes that have occurred in the business world during the past 15 years. They necessitate a change in the way people prepare their cover letters and résumés.

1. Fifteen years ago, there was not the large *proliferation of small firms*, which has been made possible by venture capital and small private investors. Today, with literally thousands of small firms whose names are unknown outside of the firm's industry or locality, and with hundreds of firms having similar names (or names differing only by a letter), *the recruiter will not recognize the name, role, or importance of your firm unless you describe it.*[4]

2. There is a continuing *horizontalization* of U.S. industry, giving a further rise in the number of firms and a mystification of their roles. U.S. industry has until recently been characterized as being vertical, with firms performing all functions in-house. For example, the automobile industry would forge its own steel, design its own cars, and so forth—within the firm. Even IBM would do all its design and development, manufacturing, and selling through the in-house organization.

We now have horizontalization. With horizontalization, independent design firms feed their output to independent system firms, which, in turn, feed their output to independent fabrication firms, which, in turn, may feed output back to the system firms for assembly of the product, which, in turn, may feed output to independent sales and distri-

---

[4] The British weekly magazine, *The Economist*, February 6, 1988, indicated that, "Since 1981, more than 19 of 20 new American jobs have been in tiny firms with fewer than 100 employees. . . . That percentage has been achieved because big firms have been running their payrolls down. Nineteen of each 20 new jobs have been service jobs. . . ." Gone are the names of well-known firms. You may have to make your firm's name known.

bution firms, which are backed up by independent installation and service firms. If your firm is not a brand name firm, but is important in the horizontal chain, describe its role in your résumé.

3. There is the *value-added reseller* sub-industry in the information industry all over the nation. This is a key new part of the information industry. There is also the new, exciting, and totally unpredictable world of *genetic engineering*. You may have to describe your industry to employers in other fields.

4. There is a variety of new college degrees and degrees created by cross-pollinization. For example, computer science is linked with a wide variety of disciplines such as history, music, and forestry; the multi-variations in the chemical, biological, and physics worlds to support genetic engineering and the new pharmaceutical domains. You should clearly state your qualifications so that the reader will understand your training.

5. There is considerable fallout from takeovers, leveraged buyouts (LBOs), mergers, or ventures that did not work (due to lack of funding, lack of management, lack of market, etc.). If you were a victim of any of these, you should explain the circumstances clearly and succinctly in your résumé so that the reader can recognize what occurred in the firm and to you. This is especially important if the event involved an undistinguished firm.

6. The *new immigrants* do not necessarily start at the bottom rungs, as their predecessors did. There are many people in industry from Asia, the Middle East, and Latin America, who received their education in universities well-known in their own country—but virtually unknown here in the United States. These new immigrants should define clearly the quality of their schools and non-U.S. professional experience.

7. Fifteen years ago, résumés were for the most part, sent out on a regional basis. Today, with the nuclear family dispersing, with industry restructuring itself, and with new centers of industry coming into prominence (beyond California and the Sun Belt) people must present themselves on a national basis. *Your school, firm, business successes, and the nature of your industry, however, may only be known in your region. Thus, you must explain and identify the quality and strength of your background in clear, definitive terms—so that the reader appreciates you as an individual.*

PART II

EVALUATING YOURSELF

This chapter will show you how to make a competitive evaluation of yourself and how to select and present your features.

A person seeking a job frequently assumes he has excellent credentials, but he probably has not compared himself to his competitors—the other qualified people—often the same people who can beat him out for the interview if he does not present himself properly and clearly. Using brand names—if you have them—can boost your value over your competition.[5]

Detailed tables are presented on the following pages. Table 2–1 is for the professional with a college degree and an already achieved career experience. Table 2–2 is for the recent college graduate. Both tables are similar in structure and enable job seekers in both categories to define their brand name attributes.

The tables are realistic starting points for your self-evaluation. They are designed to be as universal and comprehensive as possible, but they do not exhaust all the items that any individual can consider. An objective self-evaluator can expand this list.[6]

This list of items will help you identify your strong points and your weak points. Your strong points are used to identify your brand name.

---

[5] An additional observation concerning the need to *identify* your firm and background may be made if we observe where a *non–brand name* résumé *may* be used, such as in Europe. In the European business environment the elements of a cover letter and résumé are:

COVER LETTER:	Handwritten and minimal
THE RESUME:	Background: minimal embellishment
	Accomplishments: Not described, to maintain non-sales-type presentation
	Experience: sparse
	Schools: sparse

Why can résumés in Europe be shorter and less explanatory? Since there are fewer school and corporations in any one country and candidates typically seek positions in their own country, the human resource manager or the recruiter in any one nation will most likely know the reputation of any school or firm listed in the résumé. Also, unlike the corporate world in the United States, there has not been the strong growth of venture capital and entrepreneurship which has given rise to new firms. The reader of the résumé does not have to cope with undistinguished names as the U.S. reader must. (This condition may change as 1992 approaches, when there will be a significant lowering of the tariff and legal boundaries in the European Economic Community [The Common Market], which will allow an easier flow and interchange of goods, services, personnel, and corporations between the member nations.)

[6] The tables are based on the author's observations, on the *considerations* taken into account by the people performing the hiring process, from the beginning to the end of the process. These consist of many diverse factors, such as the candidate's education and qualifications and whether they are applicable to the company, the cost of interviewing, the cost of relocating and the probability that the family will agree to the relocation.

They will be featured in your cover letter and positioned in the beginning of your résumé. The weaker points may also be shown in your résumé, but you will not dwell on them or waste time or space in your introduction.

The more items you have on the upper part of your table, the better your competitive position. And the better your position, the more options you have in your job search. If most of the items about yourself appear on the lower part of the table, you have fewer options—in spite of what the books say about everyone being equal. I call these books the "pat-on-your-back" books. They sound good, but they are entirely unrealistic.

The location of any item on the charts is meant to show its value relative to other items *in the same column*. No comparisons should be made between items in *different* columns.

In order to position yourself as a brand name, use the five columns on the left of the table. (Recent graduates will find themselves referring mainly to the first two columns, until they accumulate job experience and business contacts.) To get an idea of what your place in the table means to you, examine the three columns on the right-hand side. Those columns indicate how the hiring world might perceive your potential and how you should concentrate your efforts in looking for a job.

The table will also give you some idea of *where* to look for a job—in your city or state or local region or on a national basis. This self-analysis should, as a minimum, help you cut down on mailing letters to firms that would not be likely to consider paying your moving costs.

Unless you are a very strong brand name, where you look is probably the most important part of your search. Also it is clearly easier to succeed in regions that are enjoying an economic boom than in areas where growth is slow or nonexistent.

Since your job-searching strategy is so important, let us first explore the various aspects of the table and what they mean to different people in defining their plan for looking for a job.

When you look for a job, you must select your options from a broad range of choices. For example, you can consider looking for a position:

1. *Above* your present one (e.g., regional manager, as opposed to your present branch manager position); one at your *present* level or even at a *lower* level (such as a sales manager in a branch).
2. In a larger firm than your present one, or in a smaller firm, or in one the same size.
3. With broad nationwide responsibility, or one that has only local responsibilities (or regional, North American, international, etc.)
4. In a corporation with nationwide operations and working at corporate level; or seeking to be involved only with local or regional operations; or with a firm having only local or regional operations.

Within the four cases above, you can consider whether you wish to look within your local area or consider positions outside that area, (e.g., in your region of the country, nationwide, or outside the country).

TABLE 2–1
The Professional

Corporate Affiliations	Education	Personal	Career Momentum
(Firms you have worked for or dealt with)	Ph.D. in a discipline critical to a business-growth sector.	Awards: nationally known scholastic awards (summa cum laude, Fulbright, etc); athletic; military.	Always has a steep upward movement; better than contemporaries.
Fortune 100 firms.	M.B.A.—schools such as Stanford, Harvard, Chicago, Wharton, Tuck, Fuqua, and Columbia.		Has run a true P&L.[8]
Firms presently "very up in the news."		Verifiable record as strong achiever.	
Fortune 500 firms.	Technology—Schools such as Cal Tech, Stanford, and MIT.		Is used to dealing with top decision-making executives.
Regional corporations (To seek a job outside the region, you must describe the role and products of the firm).	Ivy League schools.	Mobility minimal relocation costs.	Modest upward movement.
U.S. firms' overseas operations.	Elite, small liberal art schools such as Reed, Oberlin, Swarthmore, and Amherst.	Living in a nongrowing region.	At age 45, has not reached upper level ranks or is in a career path that is needed less and less (regulatory issues, dying industries, etc.).
Recent return to United States after a long-term stint overseas.[7]	Military academies.		
Local corporations (To seek a job outside the locale, you must describe the role and products of the firm).	Large universities whose names are usually recognizable by sports notoriety.	Many children.	
	Large universities.	Undergoing trying divorce or separation.	Is a job hopper with no noticeable advancement in professional career.
	Locally known school.		
	Partial education or noncollege education.	Age over 50.	

[7] Traditionally, this is a difficult situation. If you try to relocate to the United States, play down what you did overseas, except where it *directly* relates to operations similar to those performed in the United States.

[8] Many industries divide their business operations in such a way that they say the VP of marketing "has a profit and loss (P&L)" or that the regions also "have a P&L." I do not consider this to be a true P&L, since they do not control critical operations such as development and manufacturing.

The selection available to you among position levels, sizes of firms, and locales are many. What you select as your option(s) is based on your brand name attributes—your schools, the firms you have been with, your success, and your personal situation (size of family, age, worldliness, etc.). The table will help you make the best selection in your job search.

The column toward the right, entitled *Perception of Employers*, contains a few insights on how a potential employer may consider you. You will most likely be evaluated according to where most of your features are on the table—in its upper regions or in its lower regions.

To illustrate, consider some examples:

Example 1. The person's features fall in the upper-upper part of the table. This person can seek a position higher than his present one and can look in most parts of the country. The potential employer will consider that the person can make a valuable contribution, and he will take a risk to spend the time and money to interview the candidate and move the family.

TABLE 2–1—Continued

Business Contacts	Perception of Potential Employer	Features of the Résumé	Where to Concentrate Your Job Search
(Senior managers, decision makers, etc.)	You are seen as a potential CEO.	Emphasize brand names. Emphasize accomplishments.	Search anywhere.
(This vertical column is included to show what may be a key ingredient in the success and ease of your job search).	Opportunity awaits.	Emphasize upward movement. Emphasize any brand names.	
	You are considered an excellent commodity on job market.	Emphasize accomplishments.	
Many contacts nationwide or many in a locality or many concentrated in your business sector (>40).	You are director, vice president, or senior management potential.	Seek to identify unique features that will differentiate you from your competition: product knowledge, geographic territory, individual contributions.	Concentrate on regional opportunities (or high growth centers), and work through personal network.
	An employer outside your region may not have much interest in you.	Emphasize any brand names.	
A reasonable number (20–40).		Emphasize accomplishments.	
Some (5–20).	An employer outside your locale may not have much interest in you.	Seek to identify unique features that will differentiate you from your competition: product knowledge, geographic territory, individual contributions.	Concentrate on local opportunities (or high growth centers), and work through personal network.
Minimal number (<5).	Stick to your local territory.		

Example 2. Attributes are similar to those in Example 1 above, but this person has been at a similar level of responsibility for a number of years (5 to 10) with the same employer or with two or more employers. This person will probably not be considered for a position significantly higher than the present position. This person can consider the national job market.

Example 3. Similar to Example 2, this person is over 50 years old. This is a difficult situation—even with a good career growth. The job seeker should work through personal business contacts. Depending on present level and success this person can go national, regional, or local, but should not seek a new, large challenge without eminent success in the past.

Example 4. Most attributes are in the lower half of table. This person is under 40 and single. The best plan is to look for position in the region, in a local area, or in a high growth area, which will be defined in Part VI. This person should seek a similar or slightly higher position.

TABLE 2–2
The Emerging Professional—The Recent College Graduate

Education	Personal	Personal and Family Background	Business Contacts
Cite all schools and all degrees in beginning of résumé.	List nationally known scholastic awards (summa cum laude, magna cum laude, high scholastic point scores, fellowships, Fulbright, etc.); athletic awards; military medal.	If parents are successful professional people in a career that has prestige or relates to your career path, introduce this information discretely.	Senior managers, decision makers, and so forth.
Emphasize degree from any of the schools in top of list.			
Ph.D. in a discipline critical to a business-growth sector.	Cite any summer, part-time, or co-op jobs that relate directly to your career path.	Based on family and school activities, this person is used to dealing with top decision-making executives or top professionals.	(This vertical column is included to show what may be a key ingredient in the success and ease of your job search.)
M.B.A.—Schools such as Stanford, Harvard, Chicago, Wharton, Tuck, Fuqua, Columbia, Carnegie-Mellon, Berkeley.	List documentable events that show you as a strong achiever in schools, clubs, sports, part-time jobs, etc.	This person has had the influence of a strong mentor.	
Technology: Schools such as Cal Tech, Stanford, MIT.	Mention ability to speak foreign languages.	This person has traveled extensively on own or has lived abroad for a sustained period in course of childhood development.	Many nationwide or many in a locality or many concentrated in your business sector (>40).
Ivy League school.	Mention mobility.		
Elite, small liberal art schools such as Reed, Oberlin, Swarthmore, Amherst.	In this stage of your development, you should not have any negatives against you. Cite all the positives you can—especially when they relate to your career path, when they show your initiative and creativity, and your inclination to take charge.		A reasonable number (20–40).
Military academies.			
Large universities whose names are usually recognizable by sports notoriety.			Some (5–20).
Large universities.			
Locally recognized school.			
Partial college education.			Minimal number (<5).

I suggest that the most important positive aspects in your table are the quality of the schools you attended and whether you have had a successful upward career—preferably in a brand name firm. Having attended a well-known school will continue to have a bearing on your brand name recognition long after you have graduated. Play it for all it is worth. Some of the negative aspects that will make your search more difficult are a lack of advancement in your work career, the absence from your résumé of a recent line-management position, a preponderance of experience overseas in a role that did not relate to U.S. industry, and your age.

Note: The selection of features indicated as being "very much in your favor to advertise" is based on the reader's expected *perception* and is not meant to indicate the inherent quality of the feature. We are only indicating how you should present yourself in your selling document. Needless to say, you may have attended a small college that is little known on a national level, and yet you may be better educated than many graduates of Ivy League schools. But since the average reader of your résumé probably will not make this judgment without meeting

TABLE 2–2—Continued

Perception of Employer	Suggestions for Résumé	Where to Concentrate Your Job Search
You are seen as a potential CEO.	Emphasize brand names.	Search anywhere.
Opportunity awaits.	Emphasize accomplishments.	
You are considered an excellent commodity on job market.	Emphasize job activities that are career related.	
You are director, vice president, or senior management potential.	Emphasize any brand names.	
	Emphasize accomplishments.	Concentrate on regional opportunities (or high growth centers), and develop and work through your personal network.
	Emphasize job activities that are career related.	
	Emphasize any brand names.	
	Emphasize accomplishments.	
	Emphasize job activities that are career related.	
	Seek to identify unique features that will differentiate you from your competition: product knowledge, geographic territory, individual contributions.	Concentrate on local opportunities (or high growth centers), and develop and work through your personal network.

you, you would be wise to play up experience or accomplishments or brand name scholastic achievements such as Phi Beta Kappa, Fulbright, and the like.

Furthermore, the table has no bearing on how you might succeed in a face-to-face meeting, where personality, dress, and physical attributes may have a great effect. But remember, you will not be likely to get that chance without a strong, selling résumé.

You can develop your own more individualized table by adding features that are important to your particular industry. Think of those features that are brand names of your industry and will be immediately recognized by people familiar with the field. *Caution:* Make sure you are including on the top of your table only the items that really represent only you. Control yourself. This is not a "self-reward" game. It is a self-analysis designed to help position yourself realistically in the job market.

You should ask someone to review your table, but beware of people who want to make you feel good. Look for someone who will be objective and not worry about hurting your feelings. It may not be the most pleasant experience, but it will help you to understand how a stranger would assess your qualifications.

PART III

YOUR COVER LETTER AND RESUME

This chapter will tell you what is required for you to become a brand name. It will tell you what and where to put the facts that describe you in your cover letter and résumé (referred to as the CLR). It also suggests what you should omit, or at least play down in order to avoid using valuable space with irrelevancies and repetition, thereby diminishing your reader's interest.

When preparing your CLR, think of it as an ad agency would when it prepares a product brochure. It must give a succinct message with no irrelevancies to make someone interested enough to *consider* buying the product. Similarly, you want to get *your* message across quickly and clearly so that the reader wants to meet you.

As with an advertisement in a brochure or in a newspaper, *where* you say something is as important as *what* you say. Your best points—those that would make the reader want to call you in for an interview—belong up front. They *do not belong at the end of your "self-advertising ad space."*

The presentation consists of:

- The cover letter: *what you are.*
- The résumé: *what you are; key selling points about you—your brand name educational institution(s), well-known awards, achievements, and your most recent position.*
- Previous business experience, education, and personal matters (background and less important information about yourself).

The Cover Letter

The cover letter is your own personal statement about what you are and what you seek. It is a personal statement, different from the résumé, which is a factual history of yourself. The cover letter is not just a letter of transmittal, introducing your résumé. If you use it that way, you are wasting a precious opportunity to introduce yourself.

I believe the first information that is needed is a description of what you are. For example:

I am a marketing and sales executive with a specialty in the electric power distribution field, having worked for GE in its circuit breaker and transformer division for the past 12 years.

I have managed the definition of products, their introduction into the market place—and recently managed the implementation of a sales plan

($35 million) and the sales force of 20 salespersons in the Midwest (Iowa, Missouri, Nebraska, Kansas, and Illinois). In this position, we exceeded our original sales plan by 35 percent while not increasing the size of our sales force and accompanying expenses.

I have a B.A. in Economics from the University of Wisconsin and an M.B.A. from the University of Chicago. Both degrees were acquired under scholarship programs.

You should add an additional paragraph about the position you seek and your geographic preference. I prefer to see a statement concerning remuneration—salary, bonus and stock plans that you are used to—because it certainly does say a great deal about you. (Do not mention a country club, car, etc. These are not relevant at this stage.)

Do not introduce superfluous ideas, phony introductions, or inane reasons why you are seeking a new job. Here are some examples of what not to write as an introduction: (and people do it in many of the cover letters I receive)

Your firm was referred to me as one of the leading search firms in my field (and such letters pertain mainly to fields in which I do not specialize.)

Joe Smith referred me to you as one of the leading search firms. (It is always helpful to have a "real-name" referral. But make sure the firm you are writing to, or the search firm, knows Joe Smith. I don't know most of these "Joe Smiths," and when this is the case, it is an obvious ploy.)

After a successful career of more than 25 years with my present employer, I am considering looking for a new career opportunity. (Even if that is the case, the reader will probably infer that you are being let go. Why introduce a potentially negative thought at the very beginning?)

Mentioning Salary in the Cover Letter

Should you indicate your salary in your cover letter? I believe it is worthwhile to tell the reader of your cover letter how much you earn.

The reader sees immediately that you are an assertive and forthright person and that you know where you stand. By letting the reader know your remuneration goals, he can see whether it is worthwhile contacting you. This is especially helpful and necessary to anyone who is reading a stack of résumés that were received in response to a newspaper ad.

If you did not indicate salary and if your salary is far above the company's offering, then calling you is a waste of time. You might think that you should at least learn of the potential job, but my experience is that most people with a good career history and high hopes for the future will not consider any follow-up discussions.

People do not like being asked to take a drop in pay no matter what the "challenge." On the other hand, they do not mind being approached if the employer offers a slightly lower salary, augmented by a meaningful equity position.

Senior managers (COOs and CEOs) typically state their general salary range. This may be a manifestation of their confidence and assertiveness.

Perhaps your résumé gives the impression that you are at a higher salary level than you actually are. The potential employer may call about the opportunity. In this case, you have more to gain if he finds out that your salary is lower than the range he was planning to pay, only after he has qualified you for the job. At the outset, however, this may cause a dilemma in the potential employer's mind by evoking a number of questions:

- Why was he paid lower than his capability (as will subsequently be learned in the interviews and in the reference checking)? Did I miss something about his shortcomings in the interview? Is he misrepresenting his qualifications?
- He has the qualifications, but why was his employer paying him much less than the "market value"?
- Why did he take a lower pay at his previous job, since he does have the qualification for a higher salary?

We all deal in a market. When we buy a car, a house, or a washing machine or purchase a doctor's services, and the like, we all look for a deal, but not too much of a deal. We are leery if a service or a product has been priced too low. It is the same in hiring people.

Therefore, my recommendation is to put your salary range in your cover letter. Approach the job market in a forthright and assertive way. In that way, the best match is made.

The Résumé

The résumé consists of three parts:

Part 1. *Statement of what you are.* If you wish, in a second paragraph, you may state the position you are seeking.
Part 2. *Strong brand names features.* (See your chart, from which you define your brand name features.)
Part 3. *Other less important information.*

The elements of Part 2 include the following:

- If your college or university name is high on the brand name scale, put it here; if not, don't clutter this part. (Recent college graduates should include all college background within Part 2.)
- Mention of achievements should be short and to the point to back up what you are. To give **focus,** identify yourself clearly in terms of your unified set of accomplishments. If you can, feature your recent activities. Show what you did as a builder, a cost-cutter, a product designer, a sales manager, a turnaround manager, a staff person, a salesperson, a MIS manager, an account manager, and the like.
- State your most recent position and the accomplishments you attained in this position. (Or, if your most recent position is a dud and/or was short-lived, mention it briefly and go to previous position. You should be able to show this one strongly.)

Parts IV and V will present many examples of résumés, showing how a résumé is divided into these three parts.

Presentation Format: Accomplishments versus Chronology

During recent years, there has been a trend to depart from the commonly accepted form of résumé, showing a chronological presentation of jobs, to one that concentrates throughout on the individual's accomplishments. People frequently ask me which is the best format to use. I believe there are arguments for both types.

The purpose of your résumé is to get you an interview. What is the best way to present yourself to the reader so that he or she will make that introductory call to you?

People who read reports, graphs, and charts to evaluate the stock market and corporate performance always hope to see a rising curve. That means progress and prosperity. Plateaus and downward curves, on the other hand, distress them. These suggest stagnation and decline. There is a similar reaction to the rise, leveling out, or decline in a résumé. Thus, the best format is the one which most enhances—or ameliorates—the individual trends.

If the person's history shows a rising curve, this will be noticed more easily in a chronological format. If the career path has leveled out, perhaps the résumé can be made more interesting and enticing if accomplishments are featured. Even a downward trend or a lack of direction can be obscured by citing accomplishments.

Line positions or positions that are typically considered to be the "heart" of a business, such as sales and marketing, research, development, engineering, production manufacturing, and, of course, general management, when shown in a chronological format, can portray a sense of excitement. They show the individual taking on ever larger, more challenging tasks, creating more goods, more markets, and more revenue.

Functional positions, even when the person has performed brilliantly and has had an upward ride, rarely convey the same sense of dramatic progress. This is true for people in such fields as MIS, finance, administration, purchasing, human resources, and legal. I believe that in these areas it is necessary to develop excitement by citing unique accomplishments. These can be distributed within a chronological presentation or can make up an introductory section that lists accomplishments.

In all résumés, some form of chronological presentation is mandatory. Thus, even when the accomplishment format is used, the résumé must also show all job positions or work activities, firms, and time periods, specifying month and year, as with the chronological format. *There must not be any gaps.* In both presentations, the correspondence of the activities and dates is important, but it is more important in the accomplishment presentation. The reader can accept a brief chronology, but may wonder why you are not identifying accomplishments with job history in a coherent way. If any gap appears in the chronology and your résumé is "marginal" to begin with, the reader may conclude that you have something to conceal and may use that as a reason to no longer consider your résumé. (Later in this chapter where we provide some sample résumés, a *hybrid* résumé is presented. This format can be attractive to the person who has done well in the last position but is not necessarily interested in stressing prior jobs.)

Defining the Firm and the Position

If your position is not a brand name position (i.e., you cannot count on your reader to understand it) describe it so that the potential reader has some idea about what you do. Similarly, if your firm is not a brand name firm, describe it in terms of its sales volume, products, location, and so forth, using brand names wherever possible to identify the firm with the things the reader will recognize at once. Before you assume that the casual reader will know your firm, read again the material in Part I that discusses the quantity of firms that have developed in the United States —most of which are unknown in name and function to many readers.

If you are looking for a job in a business that is new to you, it is all the more important to describe your firm to the people you are approaching. Their being in a different industry, they will probably not recognize your firm as the brand name you think it is.

Avoid the Obvious and Avoid Repitition

Do not state the obvious. For example, if your most recent position described is VP of sales, you may describe in some detail what you did. But do not overload your résumé with activities that *any* VP of sales would do, such as hiring and training sales people, reviewing salaries, defining territories, and the like. This is an expected sales function. It should not take up space. Instead, emphasize what you accomplished in these areas.

Let us say you started as a salesman, then became branch manager, and then a regional manager. List only the titles, years, and locations, with a *minimum of description* for the lower positions. Do not repeat what you did in *each* of the lower assignments, such as "sold copiers and made 100 percent quota in first year"; "opened a new branch in Chicago, hired new salespeople, reviewed their salary." Cite only your *very significant* accomplishments in these positions, not the "givens" (what *anyone* would have accomplished in those lower positions if he eventually became the regional manager).

This advice concerning what is obvious and what is repetitious applies to any position in an organization, such as director of marketing, director of product planning, director of customer service, director of human resources, director of MIS, finance and manufacturing.

Age

Concerning your age, face it. Most employers look for people younger than 50 years. That's the way the world is. Remember that John F. Kennedy was popular primarily for his youth and vigor. Therefore, being over 50 is a handicap for most positions. The question is, should it be hidden on the résumé?

I consider that a personal decision, but I consider that the best résumé and cover letter to be one that reveals the person completely. When I receive a résumé that lacks dates, especially one that does not show the year the person received a bachelor's degree, I know the age group—over 50. And unless the person is a brand name, I usually lower my estimate a notch. This does not mean to say I would have necessarily considered the person if age was specified. With all due respect to EEO, age does count in the job market. If you feel it will count against you, there is no need to emphasize it by listing your birthdate, but it will only detract from your presentation if you omit other pertinent dates such as the year of your undergraduate degree.

What to Emphasize and De-emphasize—and Being Specific

The preparation of cover letters and résumés representing people with strong brand names and good career histories should be an easy task. Emphasize the brand names and show your success. People who do not have brand names in their background and/or do not have an exemplary career history have a more difficult task. They must work harder than the brand name person by emphasizing specific features in their background that will cause the reader to pay particular attention to their résumés. And likewise, they should consider deemphasizing those features that may be considered ordinary or irrelevant. For each optional item placed in the cover letter and résumé, ask the question, "Will this information help persuade a potential employer to call me to arrange a preinterview discussion or an interview?"

If someone at the top management level—in technology, corporate staff, MIS, and the like—talks of relatively mundane specialty or business development courses that were taken many years ago, I perceive that that person loses a notch or two in the evaluation process.

Many people dilute their presentation by citing personal features (dynamic profit-oriented executive; excellent team builder; excellent leadership qualities, etc.) which do not distinguish them from their competition, since nearly everyone says the same thing. If you do include these features, you should provide specific examples to demonstrate those traits. Make a strong presentation, emphasizing your unique strong points, but be specific. Deemphasize the points that do not truly distinguish you (and which may misrepresent you).

Do Not's

Do not include a personal photo unless you are applying for a modeling position or a sales position in cosmetics or a similar field. The employer should not be concerned with your looks.

Do not include letters of reference. They rarely say anything substantive. A thorough prospective employer will contact your references to learn of your strengths and weaknesses.

If your most recent business has been as a consultant and you have your own brochure describing your consulting operation, do not send it in with your résumé. It can confuse the prospective employer into thinking you are not really serious about a job.

Do not use nicknames in your cover letter. Write your name as you would if it were listed in the corporation's annual report. You are trying to develop a business relationship, not a friendship. If you must use a nickname, use it with no other first name. That is, do not write "Frederick (Bud) Hendricks," but "Bud Hendricks."

Do not list the names of your wife or children. There is time for the firm to learn that information.

Who Writes the Best CLRs

Résumés from different functional areas have different tones. Certain functional areas are more boring (or more exciting) than others. It behooves the individual to make the résumé lively and interesting. Brand names should help. Indicating where projects did not go well and how problems were overcome should be considered. Giving short well-phrased vignettes describing "*how* you increased sales by 40 percent," or "*how* you devised a human resource plan that decreased head count by 28 percent," interests the readers.

I observe that people who have inside *functional areas or staff areas* have résumés that are duller than those of people with outside or line positions. By *inside,* I mean *lawyers, finance people, treasurers, controllers, certified public accountants (CPAs), directors of management information systems (MIS), administrators, and human resources (HR) people.* Their résumés are hard to distinguish from one another except by the names of the firms they have worked for, the length of time they have been in the industry, and their colleges. What they did in their jobs frequently appears very similar from one person to another.

Consultants typically write interminably long, detailed résumés that are difficult and boring to read. No one has the right to bore his reader.

General managers write the best résumés. They write the shortest ones, they have the best identification of "what I am," and they show a sense of security and assertiveness. They know what they are offering.

Sales and marketing people exhibit more interesting résumés because they usually describe some growth that they have had in terms of additional territory, the products they sold, and the scope of their job.

Plant managers' résumés can be fascinating, but you have to read them well. They describe locations throughout the world and imply problems that very few of us ever face in industry—problems in manufacturing new products, starting new manufacturing facilities, union problems, economic upturns that called for quick action, and downturns that mean they had to lay off people.

Research and development (R&D) people, engineers, software, and systems people write interesting résumés, but it is often hard to tell from their résumés what they were individually responsible for. The better ones indicate what they contributed themselves and don't talk about the team effort at large.

I believe that more honesty in résumés is helpful. The way résumés are presently written gives the impression that no one ever makes a wrong decision. Wrong decisions are acceptable in today's business world. Obviously, too many of them are not. A potential employer is searching to find out whether the person is telling the whole story. By citing a minor failure or wrong decision, you may actually make people feel more comfortable with you.

Evaluating Your Resume

Here is a word about evaluating your present résumé and the one you will write in the very near future. I have been called upon by numerous people to give them guidance on how they should prepare their résumé. After reviewing the résumé and finding out what the person *really* is, as opposed to what the résumé presented, I've been known to call for major changes—to the dismay of the individuals. They defend their work by saying that their friends, family, and colleagues all thought their version of the résumé was very good.

I maintain that they got an uncritical evaluation, and, in most cases, they sought no evaluation at all. People too close to you may not be as objective in saying whether your résumé agrees with what you are in the business world. And they rarely evaluate it to determine whether it is a good selling document. Indeed, most people could not make that evaluation, even if they tried, since most people do not know what a good selling document is. A *good* selling document requires that an experienced person prepare it, and it too must undergo critical analysis.[9]

The lesson to learn is that people are not always objective in telling the truth about you. In the industrial world, defining a product and its associated literature and packaging material is a long, tedious task. It is one which requires give and take, critical analysis from objective people, changes in presentation and honesty. Try to be honest and objective with yourself about what you are representing.

It might be interesting to ask some of your colleagues or your spouse or a friend to write a paragraph that would describe you in 30 or fewer words. This description would be exclusively for your role in business and in your professional career. It would be interesting to see whether people have a unified view of you and whether it's the same view that you have of yourself.

You might also consider an evaluation by your ex-mate, your in-laws, someone at work whom you dislike (or who dislikes you), an ex-boss, your bottom-line oriented accountant who knows your W-2 as compared to the W-2s of others or a tough lawyer. They would certainly be likely to give you an unvarnished opinion.

---

[9] Being a salesperson does not mean that you know how to prepare sales literature. I have frequently seen salespeople's résumés that were terrible. Then again, many salespeople have never participated in the preparation of sales literature, but they would never dream of presenting their own firm's product as poorly as they present themselves.

PART IV

PERSONAL PROFILES—COVER LETTERS AND RESUMES

We will now show how the recommendations shown in the tables and described in Part III are applied. This is presented in Part IV and Part V as follows:

1. Part IV: The presentation of personal profiles of four individuals, followed by development of the CLRs.
2. Part V: The presentation of a series of CLRs with notations to show how they can be improved.[10]

Each of the four personal profiles is followed by a cover letter and résumé to represent each person.

It would be relatively easy to show what should be the key items to be presented in the résumé of a person with strong brand names and many accomplishments. Rather than going to great lengths for "easy" CLRs, the profiles presented here represent people with some sort of problem, such as lack of brand names or lack of a clearly successful career path. Also, we will consider people who may have been successful but whose features sound too similar to their competition and thus will call for product differentiation.

If the career situation that is described concerning the person is similar to your situation, the same approach in the CLR may be used even if your professional career path is different. That is, while the example may describe an engineer and you are a salesperson with a similar situation in your career, you may consider a similar approach.

PROFILE 1: Engineer, Designer of PC-Based Management Information Systems (MIS)

Robert Livsey, an electrical engineer, age 33, with no significant upward career rise, made a major change in his specialty a few years ago. His brand names are some of the firms he worked for and the manufacturers of subsystems he selects in his design work. Only recently has he found a career path that he truly wishes to follow.

---

[10] In most books, nice, prim, clean cover letters and résumés are shown without comments. Typically, these are suggested cover letters and résumés. Even these can be improved upon, but the ways to improve them are rarely shown. In Part V we will be seeing *both good* and *poor* cover letters and résumés and how they can be improved.

Career Summary

Robert has a B.S. in Electrical Engineering from a non–brand name school. He has been working since 1977 and has worked in four different firms.

He worked for Perkin–Elmer as a sales support engineer handling a spectrography product line. (Perkin–Elmer was acting as a distribution agency for the product, i.e., was not the developer of the product. The product line was relinquished by Perkin–Elmer and passed on to another instrumentation firm, Fischer & Porter.) Robert went along with the product, going to Fischer & Porter, working in a similar but expanded capacity as before—nothing outstanding.

This work didn't fully satisfy him either mentally or financially, so he became a sales representative for a real estate firm—a financial growth opportunity that did not pan out. Fortunately, at this stage in his career, Robert developed a passion for personal computer technology and systems, so he made a career change, becoming a salesman for BusinessLand. This combined his personal interest with his career. He performed systems analysis and defined the systems for the customers.

He was so effective in his job, selling to corporate accounts, that one of his accounts, Sony, offered him a position as a system analyst. He thrived in this position, analyzing business operations throughout the firm (accounting, legal, engineering support, etc.) and defining, purchasing, and installing the systems. (Systems consisting of IBM PCs, Macintosh, etc.) Unfortunately, the firm reorganized by decentralizing its system support team (locating them in a different region of the United States, where Robert did not wish to live) and by cutting staff at headquarters. He will now prepare his CLR.

Comparison with Charts

There are no strong features in Robert's general background that are shown on the charts. He has been employed by some relatively well-known firms, but he was not in the mainstream of growth activity (except at one time at BusinessLand). The systems he selects are made by brand name manufacturers. Since he does not have a skill that would warrant a potential employer to move him a long distance, Robert should seek a position in his locality or region. He should emphasize the features in his recent career history.

The CLR

The brand name résumé of Robert emphasizes his career interest in the PC system world. We emphasize what he is at present. Brand names are emphasized to show his acceptance by major firms. A minimal description concerning his work supporting instrumentation is expressed. Nothing is left out in his career history.

Robert's résumé is now applicable to a number of different potential job opportunities, such as working for an organization that uses PCs (in which he would have a job similar to his last one) or for a vendor firm (manufacturer, system reseller or retailer) selling to corporate accounts.

Robert M. Livsey
384 Ames Street
Caldwell, MA 01834
(617) 342 9186

Dear Sir:

I am a specialist in the solution of business problems through the use of microcomputer technology. As an example, I was the first PC Systems Specialist in the MIS department of the Sony Corporation and was the leader in the introduction of PC technology in the firm.

My career path was originally oriented to high-technology instrumentation systems working for such firms as Fischer & Porter Company and Perkin-Elmer Electronic Instruments.

In 1987 I made a career change which continues to take advantage of my strong technical capabilities, to specialize in microcomputer based information systems. I have since made significant accomplishments at BusinessLand and Sony.

I am therefore qualified for such information system positions as:
>Information Systems Manager
>Information Center Analyst
>Microcomputer Systems Manager
>Microcomputer Systems Specialist

My recent salary was $33,000. If you are interested in my qualifications please call me.

Sincerely,

384 Ames Street
Caldwell, MA 01834
(617) 342 9186

ROBERT M. LIVSEY

A specialist in the solution of business problems through the use of microcomputer technology. I define the problems with the business managers, design the systems including hardware, software, and business procedures, negotiate with vendors, install the systems, train the people, and leave in place operational business systems.

CAREER SUMMARY

Eleven years experience in systems analysis, systems design, training, technical sales, engineering, and support of various electronic systems, including microcomputer business systems, computerized data acquisition systems, and instrumentation systems. I have worked for such firms as Sony, BusinessLand, Fischer & Porter, and Perkin-Elmer.

EMPLOYMENT HISTORY

7/87 - 9/88	Sony Corporation, New York, NY

<u>PC Systems Specialist</u>

First systems specialist in firm to introduce PCs corporate-wide.

Designed and implemented microcomputer business systems including four local area networks for the Marketing, Engineering, Purchasing, Accounting, Legal, and Personnel departments. Systems installed included Macintosh, IBM classic and PS\2, Novell, Unix, and micro-to-minicomputer communications.

1/87 - 6/88   BusinessLand, New York, NY (A major retailer of PCs.)

<u>Systems Consultant</u>

Outside-sales desktop publishing specialist. Selling activities include cold calling, targeted telemarketing, seminar creation and execution, applications development, and after-sale support.

12/85 - 12/86   Self-Employed Real Estate Business

11/81 - 11/85   Ampex Magnetic Systems, Redwood, CA
<u>Technical Representative, supporting sales in New Jersey</u>
Responsible for sales and support of electronic storage recorders and instrumentation amplifiers covering the territory from Maine to Delaware. This included major organizations such as IBM's Watson Laboratory, Raytheon, Digital Equipment Corporation, and MIT.

ROBERT M. LIVSEY

EMPLOYMENT HISTORY continued

5/79 - 11/81   Fischer & Porter, Warminster, PA

Product Specialist - Marketing Department
Spectrophotometry Group

Responsibilities included technical marketing support for the direct sales force located in 11 branch offices consisting of 50% direct customer contact and 50% training and support of the sale force

5/75 - 5/79   Perkin-Elmer Intstrumentation Division, Norwalk, CT (a division of Perkin-Elmer Corporation)

Product Service Specialist - Spectrophotometry

Responsibilities included technical support and assistance to eight Dealer/Rep organizations including field service calls, training, spare parts and documentation maintenance, service bulletins, demonstrations of applications, and repair of laboratory equipment.

EDUCATION

Bachelor of Science - 1976
         Des Moines Institute of Technology; Des Moines, Iowa
           Major: Electronic Engineering Technology

Xerox Professional Selling Skills II - March 1981

PERSONAL DATA

Date of Birth: May 28,1956
Married, three children, 2, 6, and 7
Excellent health

PROFILE 2:   MIS Director

Ms. Wiley is not a top manager; her résumé will read like those of the hundreds of MIS managers that are usually on the job market if she did not follow the brand name approach.

Ms. Gerry Wiley, who is a middle-level manager of MIS, in her mid-40s, has leveled out in her career. Ms. Wiley earned a B.B.A from a state university in 1963. She has applied her skills in a variety of industries and firms and only one of the firms is a nationally known brand name. The firms have been substantial in terms of sales and profits.

Career Summary

Ms. Wiley has progressed from her introductory position in accounting to performing substantive work for each firm, as shown by titles she has had: Manager, Financial Business System; Director, Systems Programming; Director, Operations; Director, International Operations—Finance and Administration; and Director, Financial and Administrative Systems. She has held positions in various states in the United States and had a two-year stint in her latest employer's London office, where she managed the firm's European finance and administrative operation.

Since the names of her employer firms are not important, Ms. Wiley features her role and position titles in the firm. This is probably true for most MIS positions since they are for the most part similar in function (not size or scope) within most firms.

While not being a technician, Ms. Wiley has promoted the introduction of advanced technology in the organization she has worked for, implementing state-of-the-art systems with success. She showed an aptitude for this early in her career by introducing new real-time terminals when this was an innovation. Now, she stays ahead of the pack by implementing decentralized operations—taking advantage of PC and file-server technology and products. She has also been creative in hiring and training practices that have brought about substantial reduction in personnel turnover and operating costs, accompanied by increased staff productivity.

Comparison with Charts

Ms. Wiley has a modest background when we compare her features to the charts. Perhaps the only brand name feature is that she went to Ohio State University (in the middle of the chart). While she has had yeoman tasks, there is no sense of strong upward movement to make her a candidate that an employer would strongly want to hire unless she emphasizes the strong contributions she had made.

If she only talks at length about the standard activities that most MIS directors concentrate on—the size of the budget they had, the planning they did, the number of employees they managed, the

Profile continued on page 33

Ms. Gerry Wiley
862 Chelms Road
Des Moines, Iowa 50314
(515) 249 3406

Dear Director of Human Resources:

I am seeking a position within the area of MIS/Financial and Administration systems. I have twenty years' experience in this field and have held a wide range of responsibilities. I therefore am qualified for the following positions:
Director MIS
Director Systems Programming
Director MIS Operations (U.S. or Europe)
Director, Financial and Administrative Systems
Director, Planning and Development

A hallmark of my career has been to focus on two of the most important parts of a MIS business operation:
1) Improving the quality and scope of the services that are needed by the MIS system users by managing the conversion to a distributed system operation from a centralized operation; and
(2) Development of personnel. I have demonstrated the ways to introduce new and creative ways to measure the potential of new hires, to train present employers, and to upgrade their capability—all to reduce personnel turnover and increase employee productivity.

In these operations I have been the lead manager for both planning and implementation and have worked closely with major vendor organizations such as Unisys, ATT, and Computer Science Corporation.

My present salary is $83,000, plus a bonus plan of fifteen percent.

I look forward to discussing my background with you in the very near future.

Sincerely,

<u>Ms. Gerry Wiley</u>

862 Chelms Road
Des Moines, Iowa 50314
(515) 345 8798 (O)
(515) 249 3406 (H)

An MIS Director with strong development, business and international background who will bring two key strengths to any employer:

1. Planning and management to go from centralized operation to distributed systems thereby improving the quality and scope of the services that are needed by the MIS system users; and
2. Development of personnel through new and creative ways to measure the potential of new hires, to train present employers, and to upgrade their capability—to reduce personnel turnover and increase employee productivity.

Experience

3/83 - Present	**Seybold Industries, Inc.,** Des Moines, Iowa
	Manufacturer (Sales $400,000,000)
	86 - Director, Financial and Administrative Systems
	84 - 86 Director, International Operations
	86 - 84 Director, Systems Planning
7/83 - 3/83	**Auto Merchandise Company, Inc.,** Raleigh, NC
	Showroom Wholesaler of automobiles (Sales: $22,500,000)
	81 - 83 Manager, Financial Business Systems
	78 - 81 Senior Systems Analyst
4/74 - 9/78	**Whethroe & Co.,** Miami, Florida
	Wholesale Distributor (Sales: $30,000,000)
	Data Processing/Office Manager
8/71 - 2/74	Various accounting positions, including Senior Accountant, Accounting Manager, Assistant Controller.

Outstanding Accomplishments

<u>Implementation of real-time networks</u> This covered a wide range of activities such as implementation of networks within the U.S. to facilitate order-entry process, inventory control, accounts receivable and payable, purchasing, and spare parts inventory. Equipment included UNISYS, ATT, and special software developed by Computer Science Corp—all developed during the early nineteen-sixties when most operations were still doing batch processing. This successful implementation greatly increased services provided by the MIS organization.

Ms. Gerry Wiley

Recently planned and implemented a local area network strategy to be implemented within the firm's scattered operations both in the U.S. and overseas.

Personnel development Made a comprehensive study of MIS personnel evaluation and training methods that were being implemented within other major corporations within the United States. Based on the study, defined a narrow set of these programs, modified them to meet the specific requirements of the corporation, and instituted the system. The results in the first year were startling. A reduction in turnover by a factor of 5 within the first year—with this low level of turnover being maintained, in subsequent years. Productivity increased significantly and operating costs were significantly reduced.

Other Accomplishments

Directed new systems development and production systems support activities in support of foreign and domestic locations. Foreign locations included - London, Birmingham, Milan, Barcelona, and Frankfurt.

Conducted planning activities and developed long range systems plans for review and approval of Seybold's executive management—and implemented these.

Instituted a Project Control System at Auto Merchandise that included time reporting to track the status of all enhancement and maintenance projects.

Represented the MIS department in meetings with Seybold's corporate management (CEO, COO, EVP and Sr. VPs) showing how we enhanced the corporation's services while reducing operating costs. In 1987 made a presentation at annual stockholders' meeting showing how the firm is providing better services to its customers—and attracting new ones, through the expansion of its decentralized MIS functions.

Recommended and implemented a microcomputer-based project management software system which was adopted as the corporate standard.

Personal

B.B.A. University of Massachusetts (1971).
Date of birth: January 12, 1948.
Married; two children, 9 and 12.

performance tasks on time and in budget—she will not make a brand name presentation for herself.

She should emphasize (1) her contributions in promoting the introduction of advanced technology, thereby increasing the effectiveness of the firm at large and (2) her creative work in defining how to hire and train personnel—also having an impact on the firm by reducing costs. These are featured in order to differentiate her from the competition—the other people seeking positions in an MIS department with similar background, (of which there are many at any one time.

PROFILE 3: Senior Sales and Marketing Executive

Harold Bass, age 51, has leveled out in his career. He has experience in both regional and national markets with two brand name firms.

Harold Bass, a 51-year-old sales manager, specializes in the electric power systems (primary power, M-G systems, standby power, etc.) that are purchased by the construction industry for installation in factories, office buildings, and hospitals. He has worked for General Electric (GE), Power Denim (a start-up corporation), and Emerson Electric. Concentrating in central United States, he has held both sales management and staff marketing positions. He received a B.S. in electrical engineering from the University of Wisconsin and an M.B.A. from the University of Chicago.

Career Summary

Harold started with a bright future and has had moderate success. He attended excellent schools. He had advanced well in GE, but in the 1980s he was affected when GE deemphasized the power business sector. While at GE, he held both line sales management jobs (salesman, branch manager, central states regional manager) and staff positions. In the staff roles, he exercised the outlook and knowledge he obtained in his M.B.A. and in his continuing education programs at the University of St. Louis and the University of Iowa.

As GE reduced its commitment to the power business, fewer upper management positions were available. In addition, he also realized he would not be given the responsibility for a P&L—something he craved—so he joined a start up firm as VP of marketing with a good equity position.

The firm, Denim Electric, was funded by a local venture capital firm. Harold was given equity—a chance to become rich and a chance to be president if the firm succeeded. The firm specialized in a specific niche in the power field, but on a U.S.-wide market.

As with so many start-ups with a bright future, a great product, and a good team, the firm failed due to the product being late. (It could just as well have been due to a downturn in the market, the product being ahead of its time, a falling out of the VCs, undercapitalization, etc.).

Profile continued on page 37

Harold Bass
54 Old Country Road
Des Plaines, IL 60017
(708) 978 4355

Dear Sir:

I am a successful sales/marketing executive in the field of electric power systems (UPS, primary and standby power systems). The market for these systems is the construction industry, for installation in industrial and building sites. I have had vice-presidential positions with such firms as GE and Emerson Electric. I have managed major sales and service operations covering the U.S. and possess special insights into the U.S. central region from the Gulf States to the Canadian border.

I have also directed successful product programs in two major firms, GE and Emerson Electric. I was the program leader for GE's leading products, the RT-301 (in profitability, with 16 percent on sales and a market share of 34 percent), and the MG402 (sales over a five year period of $720 million) and for Emerson Electric's UPS System 14.

I have complete confidence in my ability to accept any executive position in the power field based on my experience and my academic training received at the University of Wisconsin (B.S.E.E.) and the University of Chicago (M.B.A.). My recent compensation packages have ranged between $100,000 and $125,000.

I look forward to hearing from you in the near future.

Sincerely,

Harold Bass

54 Old Country Road
Des Plaines, IL 60017
(312) 582 5834 (O)
(708) 978 4355(H)

Summary

A sales/marketing executive in the field of electronic power systems (UPS, primary and stand-by power system). Have broad range of experience in: sales management, product introduction, and product planning—gained at industry leaders— GE and Emerson Electric.

Education

University of Wisconsin   (B.S.E.E.) 1960
University of Chicago   (M.B.A.) 1962

Career History

1985-1988

Emerson Electric: <u>Vice-President, sales</u> central region. Responsible for central region sales ($78M), six branch offices and 24 salespersons. Products sold primarily to construction industry for installation in airports (Dallas--Fort Worth, Topeka), hospitals (Humana--Des Moines; St. Joseph's--Minneapolis).

Leader of special task force to finalize feature package, pricing, and introductory plan (U.S.-wide) for Emerson's UPS 14 Plan resulted in remarkable success for product—Emerson's most successful UPS product introduction, resulting in capturing 32% of UPS sales in 1987.

1983-1985

Denim Electric: <u>Vice-President sales/marketing and product planning</u>. Start up firm (sales attaining $8M), backed by local venture capital firm, with unique product for standby power system in airports. Operation plan saw potential in five years for $80M sales.

Joined in second year of operation. Product was beta tested successfully in twelve airports (Dallas--Fort Worth, O'Hare, Topeka, Champaigne, etc.). Firm could not expand due to lack of capital and product sold to Emerson Electric.

1964-1983

General Electric, Electronic Power Systems Division.
<u>Regional Director</u>, Central Region (regional sales $110M).
1980 - 1985
Provided overall leadership for sales, installation, and service for all of GE's electronic power systems.

Product sold to major construction and A&E firms such as Bechtel and Knudson for installation is broad range of major facilities (hospitals, airports, office buildings, etc.).

Harold Bass

Headed up division task force to finalize specification for the GE RT-UPS 39 and MG402, specifying features, pricing, and U.S.-wide product introduction plans.

Division Director, Market Planner 1975 - 1980

Established and directed GE corporatewide team to examine U.S.-wide fixed installation power system market. Analyzed technologies, markets, competition (U.S. and overseas).

Varied Sales/Marketing and Product Planning Positions
1964 –1975

Personal

Married with 4 married children; excellent health; 6', 190 lbs.

Date of birth: May 18, 1938.

He joined Emerson Electric, which was expanding its power system area, mainly in (uninterrupted power supplies (UPS). At the same time, Emerson was acquiring new UPS firms to add to its product lines and was consolidating. (This overall corporate strategy was not revealed or apparent to Harold at the time of hire.) After three years with one of the operations as regional VP (a sales and service management position), he was let go due to the consolidation. Now, he is engaged in a new job-seeking campaign.

Comparison with Charts

Harold attended good schools. Play this up. He did well at GE and then leveled out. While at GE and at Denim Power (but not at Emerson), he contributed a great deal to product and market strategy.

This is fine, but it is not typical for U.S. industry to hire people in a staff-type position when the industry is consolidating and when the person is 51 years old. Harold should emphasize a sales management position, citing experience in central United States, concentrating his efforts in that geographic region, backed up by strong product knowledge. A medium-sized firm could well consider him for VP of sales and marketing or a small one as the president.

PROFILE 4: Vice President of Human Resources:

Mr. Ruff has had a good career in large firms and possesses businessman qualities.

Mr. Ruff is 50 years old, and his present firm is going to be acquired. Arnold Ruff has remained at the same level within the human resource activity—a high level, but a position which is difficult to find in another major corporation. He has no brand name schools, but his firms are brand name.

Arnold is best suited for a large firm. He considers that in all his positions he has been a senior human resource executive, plus a businessman.

Career Summary

For the past 15 years, Arnold Ruff has been either a corporate director or a vice president of human resources—not much of an upward thrust, but he has performed solid work. Also, Arnold's span of control and contributions have significantly grown in his most recent position.

Many of these contributions have been within the human resource field, but Mr. Ruff has a personality and business acumen that enables him to contribute greatly to other areas within the firm, such as marketing, finance, operations, and R&D.

Comparison with Charts

Mr. Ruff has worked for brand name firms. They are members of the American and New York Stock Exchanges. He will emphasize this. He also prefers to emphasize his human resource and business accomplishments in the firm where he has been for the past nine years and to gloss over his prior work experience. The reason is that the contributions he made here are much greater than his contributions at previous firms.

He also realizes that if he only describes standard HR functions, he would not be different from his competition. (Examples of "standard" items are maintaining non-union status, redesigning cost-effective benefits and retirement programs, managing a staff that is both at corporate and at local levels.) What Mr. Ruff did that was different and distinguishing was recognizing the need to handle interpersonal problems among key executives, disseminating information concerning drugs and AIDS; making senior staff, line managers, and supervisors aware of how to handle delicate situations; and defining a strong executive succession program. He will therefore project himself in terms of his distinguishing contributions.

In addition, since he made distinguishable contributions to other operations within the business, such as marketing, finance, operations, and R&D, he will also project himself in terms of these contributions. To a senior person reviewing the CLR, this may call attention to the fact that Mr. Ruff possesses skills that can enable him to contribute to the firm at large.

Arnold H. Ruff
143 Ridge Drive
Richardson, TX
(214) 435 3256

Dear Sir:

I am responding to your ad in the October 29, 1989, issue of The Wall Street Journal. I believe that my qualifications meet the requirements you presented.

I am a senior human resource executive who has provided significant direction to major firms such as Medicorpus and Corporation XXaa. My key, recognized strength is that I contribute strongly to the general business operation—senior management, operations, finance, development and marketing—as well as providing sound and innovative leadership in the HR function. *What I have done is out of the ordinary.*

Examples of my contributions are:
- Formulated a program that resulted in two smooth CEO transitions.
- Set up a warning system to detect interpersonal problems which were affecting business outcomes and defined a method of approach to help resolve problems.
- Developed a handbook for HR and line managers to educate them about how to handle problems resulting from key social issues such as drugs and AIDS.
- Implemented a new cost effective benefits/retirement program that top management says enhanced our hiring programs and has helped us retain key employees.
- Developed a plan that shows how we should accomplish our hiring program through the use of newspaper advertising, executive search firms, and local recruiter/employment agencies.

My present salary is $145,000 plus a bonus plan of 17 percent that has been met over the past three years.

I look forward to being contacted by you.

Sincerely,

Arnold H. Ruff

1143 Ridge Drive
Richardson, TX
(214) 980 8788 (O)
(214) 435 3256 (H)

SUMMARY

A human resource executive who also contributes strongly to the general business operation—senior management, operations, finance, development, and marketing. Leads the corporation in key issue areas, such as CEO succession programs, resolving interpersonal conflicts and dealing with major corporate problems such as AIDS and drugs.

VICE PRESIDENT, HUMAN RESOURCES

Medicorpus Corporation: July 1980 to present.
An American Stock Exchange service corporation providing services to hospitals, with over 100 individual P&L branches, 15,000 employees, growing almost 175% annually through strategic expansion of product lines, new business development and internally generated growth.

As a part of senior management, was leader of a task force to define the corporation's succession program which resulted in two smooth presidential transitions.

As the senior human resource executive, responsible for directing policy and productivity through effective human resource management.

Recruiting general management and top officers—needed to keep pace with the firm's growth.

Recognized the debilitating effects interpersonal conflicts were causing at top management level and instituted a detection and counseling program which greatly reduced tension and enabled firm to exceed its profit plan.

Defined and implemented a corporate policy and training program covering AIDS and drugs. Hailed widely in the community as a "first", with program being disseminated throughout state.

Played the leading role in savings of over $1.5 million through redesign of insurance/risk management.

Prior executive experience:

Corporation XXaa. New York Stock Exchange Firm. Vice-President, Human Resources — 4/80 to 6/81.
A family-directed $900 million company in consumer goods.
A NASDAC Corporation. Corporate Director, Human Resources — 10/76 to 4/79. An international corporation establishing new directions.

A New York Stock Exchange Firm. Corporate Director, Manpower & Organizational Development — 1/70 to 10/76. A 10,000 person firm.
An American Stock Exchange. Corporate Manager, Manpower & Organizational Development — 6/63 to 1/70

Additional Achievements—for the corporation at large
(The following results were achieved <u>as a part of a team with top line executives,</u> in managing strategic change within business units.)

General Management
Developed operating and business plans, resulting in a $5 to $120 million growth. Directed organizational needs analysis to identify performance blocks and action strategies for corrections...Task force leader to a new business start-up in Hawaii: new product, process, management of assets... Implemented business teams to manage product groups, using profitability statements by line of business.

Marketing
Reversed an 8-year slide of sales through a business realignment into major market profit centers...Maintained sales dollars with 55% fewer sales personnel...Developed a "counselor" concept that increased sales three-fold.

Finance
With the CFO, assessed a 265 manned department, converting it into a major contributor with 100 fewer people...Developed project management to focus on critical business requirements by functional unit.

Operations
Implemented autonomous work groups resulting in a $550,000 cost effectiveness...80% increase in production capacity with the same number of people through automation.

Research and Development
Streamlined staffing by 25% while increasing productivity through program management.

Education
Arizona State University M.A. — 1964 (cum laude)
Administration/Supervision — Awarded Teaching Fellowship
Middle College B.S. — 1961 (cum laude) Psychology

Professional
Corporate Trustee — Middle College, New Mexico

Personal
Married, 2 married children.
Excellent health; 5'9", 160 lbs.

PART V

SETS OF COVER LETTERS AND RESUMES

This section contains cover letters and résumés that incorporate the features found in most résumés—both good and bad features. These résumés present fictitious persons. To show how the reader may be confused when the firm is not a well-known name, we sometimes use fictitious corporate names. The résumés present a broad range of backgrounds, including recent graduates and people working in sales, marketing, technology, finance, HR, MIS, and management. Not all professional and functional areas are presented by these résumés, but the reader will observe that similar features appear in most of the résumés, so that you can learn from résumés prepared for persons outside your profession.

Such features are:

- Lack of an indication of "what I am."
- Use of long sentences that provide no information showing the uniqueness of the person.
- Not using brand names to maximize effectiveness.
- Not describing a not well-known firm.
- Poor graphic presentation—either visually poor or unclear.

The résumés are ordered approximately according to assumed salary levels.

Many of the madeup résumés do not contain items dealing with personal activities: that is, civic activities, clubs, hobbies, and the like. We feel that this is mainly a personal choice. (Certain points can be made if you can say if you have a low handicap in golf, sail your 46′ sailboat, etc.)

The cover letters and résumés are annotated to point out both weak and strong points. Annotations for the cover letters are typed onto the page. Annotations for the résumés are handwritten on the résumé.

Certain of the cover letters and the résumés have been revised to present a "before" and "after" comparison. The revisions have been made according to the principles presented in this book. You can now judge which résumés you would prefer to represent you, and you can prepare your résumé accordingly.

Each cover letter and résumé is numbered to facilitate your referencing the pages in the future when you prepare your résumé. When both a cover letter and a résumé are presented, the notation at the bottom of the page is "Cover Letter/Résumé." When only the cover letter is presented, the notation is "Cover Letter," when only the résumé is presented, the notation is "Résumé." Following this notation, the word "before" or "after" appears, indicating whether the document represents the version before brand name techniques have been applied, or after, when it is the revised version. For example:

Exhibit 12–A   Cover Letter/Résumé: Before.

Exhibit 16–A   Cover Letter: Before.

Exhibit 21–C   Résumé: After.

Example 12–A

GLORIA PADGETT
2365 Simola Drive
Gainesville, FL 32613
(904) 769-5396

Good résumé in content and presentation

BACKGROUND

Recent college graduate from Tallahassee College, with B.B.A. Major in retail economics and minor in fashion technology. Upper one third of class. Have worked summers at leading Gainesville retail shopping centers for past six years, most recently assisting buyers in purchases of designer labels such as Ralph Lauren and Gorgio Armani and other U.S. and Italian brands. Seek position that will lead to senior buying responsibility.

EDUCATION

Tallahassee College, B.B.A. Major: Retail Economics
                                Minor: Fashion Technology

Senior-Year Courses

Fabric Technology
Retail Store Locations and Real Estate
Inventory: Control, Management, and Cost Analysis
Customer Psychology: Patterns and the Impact of Advertising
The Role of the Computer in the Retail Store
Economic Analysis: Examining the Spectrum of Stores (including
                    Major Department Stores, Retail Chains, and
                    the Small Boutique)

WORK EXPERIENCE

Started work career during junior year of high school (1984) and was employed each year fulltime during spring break, summer, and Christmas season.

B. SIMPSON'S, Gainsville's largest private department store.
          Assistant to the Buyer, Children's Department (1989)
          Junior Sales Clerk, Men's Furnishings   (1988)
Varied Retail Stores in Gainesville: entry level and inventory
          support positions.   (1984-1987)

PERSONAL

Born July 8, 1960
During nonschool time, live at home with my parents and two younger brothers.
Paid for 90% of tuition and personal expenses since junior year at high school.
Hobbies: Listening to local rock music groups, swimming, and reading fashion industry publications.

STEPHEN KELSO
1329 Kenosha Heights
Racine, Wisconsin 53412
(414) 470-9857

Good résumé in presentation and content.

But needs statement to say "What I am". *

EDUCATION **UNIVERSITY of WISCONSIN**, Madison, WI
Candidate for Bachelor of Political Science Degree.   August 1990
Political Science Major; current GPA. 3.1; Dean's List, Fall 1989, Spring 1990

SMITHTON PREPARATORY SCHOOL, Beloit, WI

WORK EXPERIENCE **OFFICE OF THE ENVIRONMENT**, Madison, WI   Spring 1989
Reviewed recent U.S. Congressional legislation to determine potential
impact on Wisconsin's water resources.

CHICAGO BOARD OF TRADE, Chicago, IL   Summer 1989
Research Intern to determine impact of recent investigations into commodity
operations and their impact on the growth potential of the region.

RACINE FARMERS LAND BANK   Summer 1988
Made daily briefing to the President and the Vice President of sales on
trading activities in the region's commodity and capital markets.

UNIVERSITY of WISCONSIN ANNUAL FUND, Madison, WI   Spring 1988
Telemarketing representative for alumni solicitation.

OFFICE OF U.S. SENATOR PAUL SIMON, Springfield, IL   Summers 1986-1987
- Assistant to office manager. Assisted in broad range of activities:
  Prepared responses to constituent correspondence; reviewed state
  legislature's plans that would affect national level.

- Personal responsibility: Guided two university consulting groups
  (University of Chicago and National College of Education) in their
  study of allocation and impact of federal funds on four states
  (Illinois, Missouri, Ohio, and Wisconsin) over period of past 20
  years.

CAMP HHH, Nanakan Lake, Minn.   Summer 1986
Camp Counselor.

SOFTWARE SKILLS   Lotus 1-2-3, dBase III, Microsoft WORKS, and BASIC.

EXTRA-CURRICULAR ACTIVITIES **University Theatre Advisory Committee** — Undergraduate Representative.   1990
Assisted in evaluation of candidates for new music director.

Student Advisor, Group Leader for freshman orientation.   1987-1990

References furnished upon request.   *— not needed*

Do not use bold type for unimportant items.

* If 'What I am' statement is missing, reader may be confused by list of varied activities — and may infer that the student lacks focus.

EXHIBIT 1–B   **Résumé (Recent College Graduate): BEFORE**   **45**

STEPHEN KELSO
1329 Kenosha Heights
Racine, Wisconsin 53412
(414) 470-9857

BACKGROUND

Recent College Graduate from University of Wisconsin, with **B.A.** in Political Science. Will eventually continue studies to obtain law degree, but presently wish to be paralegal in large law firm engaged in corporation law. Have worked in many environments to develop insights into the key corporate issues of the 1990s: **Environment**, with Wisconsin State Office of the Environment, Madison, WI; **Legislation**, with the Office of U.S. Senator Paul Simon; and **Trade and Business** with the Chicago Board of Trade.

EDUCATION	**UNIVERSITY of WISCONSIN**, Madison, WI Candidate for Bachelor of Political Science Degree Political Science Major; current GPA. 3.1; Dean's List, Spring 1990.	August 1990
	SMITHTON PREPARATORY SCHOOL, Beloit, WI	
WORK EXPERIENCE	**STATE OFFICE OF THE ENVIRONMENT**, Madison, WI Reviewed recent U.S. Congressional legislation to determine potential impact on Wisconsin's water resources.	Spring 1989
	CHICAGO BOARD OF TRADE, Chicago, IL Research Intern to determine impact of recent investigations into commodity operations and their impact on the growth potential of the region.	Summer 1989
	RACINE FARMERS LAND BANK Made daily briefing to the president and the vice president of sales on trading activities in the region's commodity and capital markets.	Summer 1988
	UNIVERSITY of WISCONSIN ANNUAL FUND, Madison, WI Telemarketing representative for alumni solicitation.	Spring 1988

OFFICE OF U.S. SENATOR PAUL SIMON, Springfield, IL, Summers 1986-1987
- Assistant to office manager. Assisted in broad range of activities: Prepared responses to constituent correspondence, review state legislature's plans that would affect national level.

- Personal Responsibility. Guided two university consulting groups (University of Chicago and National College of Education) in their study of allocation and impact of federal funds on four states (Illinois, Minnesota, Ohio, and Wisconsin) over period of past 20 years.

	CAMP HHH, Nanakan Lake, Minn. Camp Counselor.	Summer 1986
SOFTWARE SKILLS	Lotus 1-2-3, dBase III, Microsoft WORKS, and BASIC.	
EXTRA- CURRICULAR ACTIVITIES	**University Theatre Advisory Committee** — Undergraduate Representative. Assisted in evaluation of candidates for new music director.	1990
	Student Advisor, Group Leader for freshman orientation.	1987-1990

An Open Letter to Recent College Graduates

I have observed that many of the résumés I see from recent college graduates lack a focus or an expression of "what I am." I observe this among all levels—two-year community colleges, four-year universities and even among those with a recent master's degree. This may be due to a variety of factors: lack of sufficient exposure to the business world, lack of a guidance person (a teacher, a parent, a mentor), or just the fact that the person does not know what he or she wants to do.

In any event, a recent graduate *can* define for her or himself "what I am." The following are examples of "what I am" to help you if you find this identification process to be difficult. These examples can be the basis for your cover letter and your "what I am" statement on your résumé.

Most of these examples are "lean examples." They do not necessarily indicate extracurricular activities. They are built primarily around school and personality. If you have job-related activities from nonschool work, describe these. Or you may have non job-related brand name features (lived abroad for a period, know a foreign language, won 4-H awards, studied under a world-famous teacher, etc.). Consider including them.

> I have recently obtained my B.A. in English at New Mexico State University and now plan to enter the business world. I majored in the American psychological novel and this, coupled with my desire to work with people, enables me to make a contribution to your firm as an entry level person in a broad range of activities, including sales, human resources, documentation and training.

> I recently received my two-year certificate at Hawthorne State Community College, majoring in community affairs. I selected this specialty since I have always had a keen interest in these activities and in the well-being of any community I have ever lived in. This goes back to my childhood years (active in the Scouts, 4-H, and Red Cross, for example). I wish to continue this within a corporate or a municipal organization.

> I have recently completed an B.S. in Biology, with an emphasis on insects, at Arkansas State University. I decided to concentrate on insect biology because the subject fascinates me, and it allows me to work in a laboratory environment and be part of a team of researchers.

The two résumés presented above, 1-A (Padget) and 1-B (Kelso) are examples of how a statement of "what I am" immediately presents the person. They are interesting to examine since the persons are decidedly different, and they both need that statement.

The first résumé, 1-A, is an example of a student who might have received her degree with no outstanding education or work-related achievements. But now is the time she must seek a position. She must at last identify herself.

For probably the first time in her life she will have to say to the outside world "what I am". Thus the résumé is a straightforward presentation introduced by a "unique statement."

Résumé 1-B is very different. It represents a person who has been on the march, in school, in extracurricular activities, and in summer and part-time jobs. Obviously this is a high-potential person. Note that this résumé lacks a statement of "what I am" and therefore shows a lack of focus or a lack of direction. We might go so far as to say that 1-A is a better presentation of a person than 1-B.

Now is the moment of truth. A statement of "what I am" *must* be included. (This is hard work for most people, including most experienced professionals.) Without such a statement the recipient of the résumé may be confused by the long list and therefore not give the candidate serious attention.

Sincerely,

Allan Karson

Good overall résumé in content and presentation.

MARGUERITE CUOMO

| 4708 Kendall Lane | Bethesda, MD 20817 | (301) 725-0917 |

<u>OBJECTIVE</u>

Overview is better than objective. 'Objective' is too limiting.

A finance or marketing position in a multinational financial institution that will enable me to apply my understanding of financial engineering and international cultures. I seek an opportunity that will expose me to diverse areas of planning and analysis. I would eventually like to apply my language and intercultural skills overseas, preferably in Italy or England.

<u>EDUCATION</u>

Can be strengthened with more features on background.

GEORGETOWN UNIVERSITY, Washington, D.C. 1988-90
M.B.A., Finance and Marketing, GPA 3.7.

UNIVERSITY OF BOLOGNA, Bologna, Italy 1987-88
One-year course in International Business, concentrating on implications of 1992 changes to EEC.

NORTH CAROLINA STATE UNIVERSITY, Raleigh, NC 1986-87
Concentration in Finance, Economics, Business; Special Honors GPA 3.6.

MOUNT ANDREWS COLLEGE, Macon, GA 1982-86
B.A., Economics, Italian: Cum Laude; GPA 3.5.

<u>INTERNATIONAL CULTURAL BACKGROUND</u>

•Fluency in Italian and modest conversational capability in Spanish.
•International Fiat Award Program, Italy (1987-88).
•Semester abroad, Rome, Italy: language, history, culture (1985).
•Italian Family Abroad program: one month with host family in Italy (1981).
•Lived with my family in Italy, England and Spain—one year in each country.

<u>NON-WORK-RELATED ACTIVITIES</u> ← *Good title*

International Business Society: President, International Activities (1988-89).
North Carolina State: International Banking Trends writing award in Economics (1987).
Stage Manager, Mount Andrews College Theater Group (1985-86).

Brand name: Place up front. <u>WORK EXPERIENCE</u>

MOTOROLA COMMUNICATIONS PRODUCTS DIVISION, May 1989-Aug. 1989.
Systems Analyst (summer internship)
Conducted analysis of relationship between local banking organizations (flexibility, size, government control, etc., and success of Motorola product line in various areas, including the Mediterranean, Central and Northern Europe, and the Middle East. Developed extensive contacts with diverse financial groups, diagnosed common trends, and predicted performance.

<u>PERSONAL</u>

Date of birth: January 12, 1964; single; excellent health.

EXHIBIT 2-A **Résumé (Recent M.B.A. Graduate): BEFORE** 49

4708 Kendall Lane   Bethesda, MD 20817   (301) 725-0917

OVERVIEW

Recent MBA graduate from Georgetown with strong skills in international business and finance. Have lived and studied in Europe and speak Italian fluently. I seek a marketing or finance position in a multinational financial institution that will enable me to apply my understanding of financial engineering and international cultures. I seek an opportunity that will expose me to diverse areas of planning and analysis. I would eventually like to apply my language and intercultural skills overseas, preferably in Italy or England.

EDUCATION

GEORGETOWN UNIVERSITY, Washington, D.C.   1988-90
M.B.A. Finance and Marketing,   GPA 3.7.

UNIVERSITY OF BOLOGNA, Bologna, Italy 1987-88
One-year course in International Business, concentrating on implications of 1992 changes to EEC.

NORTH CAROLINA STATE UNIVERSITY, Raleigh, NC 1986-87
Concentration in Finance, Economics, Business, Special Honors GPA 3.6.

MOUNT ANDREWS COLLEGE, Macon, GA 1982-86
B.A., Economics, Italian: Cum Laude GPA 3.5.

WORK EXPERIENCE

MOTOROLA COMMUNICATIONS PRODUCTS DIVISION, May 1989-Aug. 1989
Systems Analyst (summer internship)
Conducted analysis of relationship between local banking organizations (flexibility, size, government control, etc. and success of Motorola product line in various areas, including the Mediterranean, Central and Northern Europe, and the Middle East. Developed extensive contacts with diverse financial groups, diagnosed common trends and predicted performance.

INTERNATIONAL CULTURAL BACKGROUND

•Fluency in Italian and modest conversational capability in Spanish.
•International Fiat Award Program, Italy (1987-88).
•Semester abroad, Rome, Italy: language, history, culture (1985).
•Italian Family Abroad program: one month with host family in Italy (1981).
•Lived with my family in Italy, England, and Spain—one year in each country.

NON-WORK-
RELATED ACTIVITIES

International Business Society: President, International Activities (1988-89).
North Carolina State: International Banking Trends writing award in Economics (1987).
Stage Manager, Mount Andrews College Theater Group (1985-86).

PERSONAL

Date of birth: January 12, 1964;   single; excellent health.

Mr. Joseph Calway

Director of Human Resources

Medway-Pacific Container Manufacturing Corporation

San Francisco, CA 94101

Dear Mr. Calway:

I am currently completing an M.B.A. at the University of California at Berkeley with a concentration in International Banking and Finance and am looking for a position within the international finance operations of your firm dealing with the Pacific Rim. I believe that working for Medway-Pacific would be mutually advantageous.

If you are seeking a person with my experience and career goals, please do not hesitate to call me. I thank you in advance for your consideration.

Very truly yours,

Vincent Fidelio

A clear cover letter, but it neglects to show that the person has work experience in a brand name bank in its Pacific Rim operations, hands-on experience in MIS within the banking environment and in a mid-sized brand name retail firm, and has had some management experience.

Mr. Joseph Calway
Director of Human Resources
Medway-Pacific Container Manufacturing Corporation
San Francisco, CA 94101

Dear Mr. Calway:

I am currently completing an M.B.A. at the University of California at Berkeley with a concentration in International Banking and Finance and am looking for a position within the international finance operations of your firm dealing with the Pacific Rim. I believe that my working for Medway-Pacific would be mutually advantageous.

I believe I am ready to take on such a position because I have worked for the Pacific Rim operations of the Bank of America, dealing with a data base describing the industrial and financial organizations active in that region. I manage a small team responsible for the development of that data base. I have done that for the past four years while obtaining my M.B.A. This experience at Bank of America has given me insights into the activities of the region.

In addition to the Bank of America experience, I have acquired modest management and MIS experience while managing ten persons responsible for MIS operation at BusinessLand stores.

While my experience is directly applicable to MIS or data base applications dealing with the region, I would like to expand my horizons by working in your firm's operations handling export-import or financial control and analysis.

If you are seeking a person with my experience and career goals, please do not hesitate to call me. I thank you in advance for your consideration.

Very truly yours,

Vincent Fidelio

EXHIBIT 3–B   Cover Letter/Résumé (M.B.A. Graduate-to-Be with Business Experience): AFTER

VINCENT FIDELIO

220 Worth Street   Oakland, CA 94603   (415) 458-2112

OVERVIEW

Good résumé in content and presentation

M.B.A from the University of California at Berkeley in international business and banking. Have four years experience as data base manager for Bank of America, concentrating in Pacific Rim operations. Have also analyzed financial and industrial operations in leading and emerging industrial countries such as Hong Kong, Taiwan, South Korea, Singapore, and PRC. Seek position in export-import or financial control and analysis in Pacific Rim industrial firm.

Shows Clearly "What I am" using brand names.

JOB EXPERIENCE

Bank of America, Pacific Rim Operations   1986 - present
Data Base Manager
Responsible for managing database of the Bank America's multinational clients. Have a staff of four persons who develop and edit programs for database management; manage all phases of publishing and disseminating the data base within all international operation centers of the bank. Information consists of both public and private information (SEC filings, special projects, credit reports, contact reports.)—a proprietary and a highly confidential data base. Security access control and dissemination are key operating aspects of the system design.

Staff Analyst
Assisted a survey of data management needs of loan officers dealing with Pacific Rim firms and operations. Activities included questionnaire development, database development and updating, analysis of questionnaire results, and preparation of final report for the data management committee. The survey is used to determine budgetary allocations for future data management expenditures within the bank's San Francisco Pacific Rim operation.

Good. Shows business knowledge of Pacific Rim.

Businessland Computer Stores, Berkeley, CA   1983 - 1986
Manager and Assistant Director of Operations
Responsible for the operation of computer systems for four locations of Businessland, including over 2,000 items, suggesting changes according to the applicability of the programs designed for store presentations; coordinated the sales operation of computer systems. Responsibilities included managing 10 store employees and orienting and training sales personnel in the four stores on computer inventory control system.

Good, recent management experience.

Started as sales person, then assisted in starting data base operation. ← *Good*

EDUCATIONAL BACKGROUND

Bachelor of Arts, The University of California at San Francisco, 1983; English and history major; Minor in oriental music; 2.9 average.

M.B.A. candidate in International Business and Banking, University of California at Berkeley. Expect to complete M.B.A. program, spring 1990.

PERSONAL

Born: July 19, 1961.   Single, with excellent health.
Enjoy sailing, hiking,and listening to Oriental music.   Student of Mandarin Chinese.

You are members of a large, growing population. You may be a person who presently holds a position within a firm, or you may have been working as an independent consultant and you are seeking a more stable, permanent position. I wish to let you know that many of the résumés I receive from your colleagues do not follow good business practices, thereby making their job search more difficult.

The résumés are frequently too long. They may contain exhaustive lists of all your experience with software, hardware and computer languages—but do not identify you as the special individual you are. Independent consultants too frequently overload their résumé with details and do not focus on key issues.

Your broad knowledge and the demand for you in the marketplace do not exempt you from preparing a résumé that presents you as the professional you are.

Two representative résumés are presented below to show what is unacceptable. They are followed by improved versions.

Sincerely,

Allan Karson

Poor presentation. Needs better identification of positions, roles, and firms.

Poor layout

ARTHUR M. GLASSBURG, 555-B Alameda, San Jose, CA 95101, HOME (408) 347-1959

Education   B.S. Computer Science, Colorado State, 1975; 14 years' experience in data systems industry.

Inadequate way to express career

Positions   Designer of software, team leader systems analyst, programmer, trainer. *must say "What I am."*

EXPERIENCE

As are thousands of other programmers. Too broad.

8/86 - Present: Consultant to IBM. *← Where in IBM?*
Lead a team producing code fixes and enhancements to the IBM DBMS IV. Required *Must show focus*
knowledge of VMS operating system design and IBM Assembler language.
Managed a team of four people, making modifications to the IBM file server/TP system
TSERV. The system is to interface with a remote DEC UNIX based system. This required
a knowledge of TSERV's internals, UNIX, file server, and products of other vendors and
VMS.

6/82 - 4/86: Keycomp, a San Jose software consulting firm.
Developed products for the IBM 3033.

This is most recent work. Expand upon it

The content may be good, but who will read it? Divide into segments.

Example: SpaceSaver (a memory compression product)—designed and developed a
significant amount of the software. This required a knowledge of PC/MS DOS internals
and data handling techniques. Designed and developed all software (dBase accelerator).
Performed code testing. The programs were written in both C and a dialect of BASIC.
Investigated MVS/XA internals for the development of an IBM 3033 to interface with and
operate on the VSAM file access systems.
Maintained and enhanced an interactive telecommunications monitor similar to TIPS but
optimized for smaller networks; 1 to 40 terminals with single and multiple mainframes
using IBM Assembler language. Required a knowledge of all IBM communications
protocols.
Designed a system interfacing 3Com, Banyan, and Convergent systems to work on special
version of Ethernet.

3/81 - 10/82: Independent consultant. *← To whom?*
Designed and wrote file server system for a DEC VAX system using Assembler.
Modified a VAX to run with a special multiprocessor machine, through remote
communication system (Telenet), X.25, and local controllers (Motorola XRX-4) for a
new factory floor shop control system.

3/78 - 2/81: Worked for Digital Equipment Corporation in Columbus, Ohio.
As a senior software designer, designed and wrote (1) telecommunications package and
(2) an inventory control system.
As a senior software analyst, developed and presented courses on programming,
communications, and data base management.

Very uninviting presentation. Lacks space between jobs and needs to highlight position titles, which are needed to guide reader to important features.

EXHIBIT 4–A   *Resumé (Computer Programmer): BEFORE*   **55**

9/75 - 1/78: NCR Corporation

Programmer/analyst working on interfacing special inventory control terminals, point of sale (POS) terminals, and remote asynchronous simple terminals (printers, card readers, time clocks) to provide major local customers with integrated systems. Programs written in "C" and Assembler. Eighty-five major terminal stations, numerous supervisory positions, with Ungermannn-Bass LANs working through Ohio Bell dedicated system. *— History. Could be shortened.*

Projects	O.S. Internals:	Designed and wrote extensions to VM for IBM.
	Data Compression:	Designed and wrote a PC data compression product.
	Data Base :	Designed and wrote an information retrieval system for a bank.
		Enhanced and amended INTERCOM (a TP monitor).
		Designed and interfaced between VAX and Telenet/XRX-4 micro.
	Communications:	Designed and wrote a VIDEOTEX system for IBM.
		Enhanced and amended INTERCOM (a TP monitor).
	Office Systems:	Designed and wrote a IPlus for IBM.
	File Server:	Designed and wrote multicluster system on VAX interfacing with 3Com units.
		Modified a Banyon system to operate with National Semiconductor chip for file/telecom transfer system.
	Training:	Prepared and presented varied computer programming courses.

Present this list as a dignified list. Give it a title and a page of its own.

Systems		PC/MS-DOS, VM/CMS, OS1, OS2, MVS, MVS/XA, UNIX Ethernet, DEC NET, X.25.
Machines	Mainframes:	IBM-370, IBM-3033, IBM-308x, Unisys mid-range.
	Minis:	DEC PDP-11. VAX, Tandem (some), HP 3010, Convergent.
	Micros:	IBM-PC, IBM-PC/AT, MacIntosh.
	File Servers:	3Com and Banyon.
Languages		Fortran, C++, C, ADA, BCPL, Pascal, Lisp, APL, Cobol, SAS, BASIC.

Needs personal information so reader has overall picture: Such as date of birth, family status, etc.

555-B Alameda   San Jose, CA 95101   (408) 347-1959 (home)

OVERVIEW

Software development engineer and project leader with extensive operating, data base, and telecommunications system experience. (Examples: VAX, VMS, UNIX, LAN's, DBMS IV). Have worked for computer manufacturers: IBM, DEC, and NCR.

Installed communication and manufacturing systems for end users. Possess first-hand knowledge of wide range of third party products and services, including 3COM, Banyon, Convergent, Telenet, and Motorola. Seeking project management position with computer manufacturer, software development firm, or VAR.

EXPERIENCE

Computer Science Corporation   **8/86-Present**

Contract Consultant to IBM Santa Theresa Laboratory. The Santa Theresa Laboratory has prime responsibility for DBMS development and enhancements worldwide.
Provide team leadership and technical services, working as integrated member of the IBM development laboratory. Lead a team of four professionals producing code fixes and enhancements to DBMS IV, the key IBM data base product. Develop project schedules and budgets, work with product managers to determine new features and problem areas. Requires knowledge of DBMS, VMS operating system design, and IBM Assembler language.

Managed a team of four people, making modifications to the IBM file server/TP system TSERV. System to interface with a remote DEC UNIX based system. Required a knowledge of TSERV's internals, UNIX, VMX, file servers, and products of other vendors.

Keycomp, a San Jose software consulting firm.   **6/82-4/86**

Software Development Engineer
Developed products for the IBM 3033. Products include *SpaceSaver* (a memory compression product). Designed and developed a significant amount of the software. Required a knowledge of PC/MS DOS internals and data handling techniques. Designed and developed all software (dBase accelerator). Performed code testing. Written in both C and a dialect of BASIC.

Investigated MVS/XA internals for the development of an IBM 3033 to interface with and operate on the VSAM file access systems.

Maintained and enhanced an interactive telecommunications monitor similar to TIPS, but optimized for smaller networks, up to 40 terminals. Required knowledge of most IBM communications protocols.

EXHIBIT 4–B   Resumé (Computer Programmer): AFTER   57

Arthur M. Glassburg (cont.)

Designed a system interfacing 3Com, Banyan, and Convergent systems to work on special version of Ethernet.

Independent Consultant to Maxman Toy Corporation　　　**3/81-10/82**

Designed and wrote file server system for a DEC VAX system using Assembler. Modified VAX to run with a special multiprocessor machine, through remote communication system (Telenet), X.25, and local controllers, the Motorola XRX-4, for a new factory floor shop control system.

Digital Equipment Corporation, Columbus, Ohio　　　**3/78-2/81**

Senior software designer　　　1979-1981
Designed and wrote (1) telecommunications package and (2) an inventory control system.
Senior software analyst　　　1978-1979
Developed and presented courses on programming, communications, and data base management systems.

NCR Corporation　　　**9/75-1/78**

Programmer/analyst
Project: NCR system product to provide integrated information-capture systems
Interfaced special inventory control terminals, point of sale (POS) terminals and remote asynchronous terminals (printers, card readers, time clocks). System consisted of eighty-five major terminal stations, numerous supervisory positions and Ungermannn-Bass LANs.

EDUCATION AND AFFILIATIONS

B.S. Computer Science, Colorado State, 1975.
Member of:　　ACM Computer Architect Group
　　　　　　　IEEE Data Communications Group.

PERSONAL

Born January 19, 1954
Married; three children, ages 2, 5, and 8
Relocation presents no problem.

Arthur M. Glassburg (cont.)

SUMMARY OF SPECIFIC PRODUCTS, SOFTWARE, AND SYSTEMS

Projects   O.S. Internals: Designed and wrote extensions to VMS for IBM.

Data Compression: Designed and wrote a PC data compression product, *Spacesaver*.

Data Base :   Designed and wrote an information retrieval system for a bank using DBMS IV.

Enhanced and amended INTERCOM (a TP monitor).

Designed and interfaced between VAX and Telenet/XRX-4 micro.

Communications: Designed and wrote a VIDEOTEX system for IBM.

Enhanced and amended INTERCOM (a TP monitor).

Office Systems: Designed and wrote a IPlus for IBM.

File Server: Designed and wrote multicluster system on VAX interfacing with 3Com units.

Modified a Banyon system to operate with National Semiconductor chip for file/telecom transfer system.

Training: Prepared and presented varied computer programming courses.

Systems   DBMS IV, PC/MS-DOS, VM/CMS, OS1, OS2, MVS,MVS/XA, UNIX, Ethernet, DEC NET, X.25.

Machines   Mainframes: IBM-370, IBM-3033, IBM-308x, Unisys mid-range.

Minis: DEC PDP-11. VAX, Tandem (some), HP 3010, Convergent.

Micros: IBM-PC, IBM-PC/AT, MacIntosh.

File Servers: 3Com and Banyon.

Languages   Fortran, C++, C, ADA, BCPL, Pascal, Lisp, APL, Cobol, SAS, BASIC.

EXHIBIT 4–B—Continued   59

Jonathan Peters   1402 13th Ave., Revere, MA 02151   Home Phone (617) 221-1787

BACKGROUND:

Poor presentation. Too long. Lacks focus. No one will read this. Must say "What I am" in clear and succinct way.

I have been in the computer industry since 1970 and am experienced in the management of division, departmental and branch computing systems for the legal, insurance and financial, manufacturing, and telecommunications fields. Have managed the definition, acquisition and test of computer systems and data center design and installation. Specialize in the Unisys and IBM mid-range systems. Managed installation and operation of networking, utilizing file servers, LAN's, PBX systems (SL-1, BXT and ATT's systems), X.25 protocols, 9.6 KBS/64KBS/T-1 multiplexers, SDL, ASYNC, BISYNC, and IBM/SNA environments. Experienced programmer/analyst and manager for COBOL programming in IBM, Unisys and DEC mainframe environments. Like equally the challenges met as a program manager, system administrator, information center manager, and telecommunications manager.

EDUCATION:

B.S., Industrial Management
University of Texas, Austin, Texas   *← Date*

HARDWARE:

Unisys mid-range
IBM PC/XT, PC/AT and clones
IBM 3081K, 3084Q, 3090 200E
IBM SNA/RJE, SNA/3270 gateways
DEC VAX 8650,8700, VAX clusters
DEC PDP-11/4.5 with special telecom mods
DEC Ethernet controllers and terminal servers
MacIntosh SE and II
Timeplex Link 1 T-1 multiplexers
Racal Milgo and Codex (modems, DEConnect)
NCR Tower
File Servers: 3COM and Banyon
Wang and CPT word processor
Communication Producer
Novell-based LAN

The list of hardware, software, and languages (next page) should go on a seperate page. (Consider that this list is similar to the "list of publications" that a person in research would append to his/her résumé.)

SOFTWARE:

DECNET
VAX/VMS
X.25
OS/VS2, MVS and MVS/XA
X.400
JES2, JES3
IBM SNA
MS/DOS and PC packages
Ethernet
UNIX
Oracle RDB
FFDI and Sonet specification

EXHIBIT 5–A   Résumé (Computer Programmer): BEFORE

LANGUAGES:	ADL
	COBOL
	FORTRAN
	C++
	SAS
	JCL

Place on one page with hardware and software.

EXPERIENCE:

1982-Present   Sentinel Life Insurance Company, Boston, MA

Poor presentation. Too long. All of this is actually interesting, but no one will read it. Should be presented in clearly defined segments, such as responsibility, duties, problems, features, environment and solutions.

Program Manager (1987-present) responsible for managing the complete corporate forecasting and sales analysis system that incorporates advanced word processing and services over 500 users in the actuarial, financial sales and human resources areas. Implemented additional network facilities (including T-1 and special microwaves), which provided more centralized control with an increase in E-mail transfers across the network. This environment consisted of a set of IBM computers, linked by a nationwide network provided by Northern Telecom SL-1 equipment Timeplex multiplexers and Codex modem and locally by a Novell LAN. Duties include system administration, configurations, network optimization, third party vendor evaluations, and the network users' primary interface/liaison for data processing. Security duties include password updates, user ID codes and control lists, setting logical and physical attributes, and maintaining a file system protection scheme. IBM/SNA/RJE installations for branch sites and IBM/SNA/3270 for the remote sites. Interface directly with the user groups/actuaries, legal, financial. Other duties consist of working with ATT's nationwide network through their network manager, introducing ISDN to the Voice Communications Manager and to the use of the Northern Telecom Digital PBX switch as a backbone for voice-over data integration, and research new IBM PC/AT terminal emulation products for PC to Host Communications.

Internal Consultant (1980-1982) responsible for initiating and producing for the following research projects dealing with actuarial rates:

Good

*   Design and development for update system for data base tables (actuarial tables, individual insurance policy results).

*   Developed corporatewide actuarial database conversion procedure to our product planners.

*   Investigated techniques and systems to evaluate the data base to be maintained using real-time data.

*   Instituted a system and procedures whereby we monitored system, software, and application software performance.

EXHIBIT 5–A—Continued   61

1976-1980   United Telecommunications, Kansas City, MO

Network Administrator for a special customer dedicated network, was responsible for managing the project's node IBM and Unisys. This system executed a "C" language communications package serving a base of twenty-one firms. Managed the implementation of data center, including hardware and software, procedures, telcom systems and personnel hiring and managing. Performed administration duties, consisting of controlling hardware and software inventories, negotiation for vendors with equipment, approving standard and extra maintenance requests. Worked closely with the programming staff to provide guidance in key communication areas such as HDLC, X400, ASYNC, X.25, and Ethernet LANS. The system tied into Telenet, Tymnet, and international record carriers (IRCs).

Same remarks as above. Needs Segmentation to make it readable.

1974-1976   McDonnel Douglas, St. Louis, MO

Operations Manager responsible for managing the firm's aircraft data base analytic system serving over 1000 internal users and 350 aircraft user firms on an international network. Had responsibility of managing a 12-node VAX cluster system that interfaced directly with four mainframes running MVS and MVS/XA. Served as an internal consultant to telecommunications department and assisted in the design, development, and installation of the X.25 portion of the corporate private line network.

Contains repetitive information

Ancient History. Shorten.

Previous Positions

Technical Specialist for a legal firm, planning and implementing the installation of special display terminals (CPT and WANG) and terminal controllers for the corporate contract facility. Designed and implemented recovery procedures for the terminal system serving the corporate department.

Technical Specialist/Programmer Analyst for a systems consulting firm specializing in factory automation. Was responsible for all technical support and operations of the customer service operation. Also performed modifications to primary software, executing on both UNIVAC minicomputer and IBM mainframe. Other conversions included an IBM system, the modification of a customized MRP system to run on a UNIVAC minicomputer.

Identify firms and dates.

Need personal information such as date of birth, family status — to give total picture of person.

Jonathan Peters

1402 13th Ave.   Revere, MA 02151   (617) 221-1787

BACKGROUND: <u>Program Manager, System Administrator, Information Center Manager and Telecommunications Manager</u>. Have managed major computer and communication systems for Sentinel Life Insurance, United Telecommunications, and McDonnel Douglas for legal, insurance, financial, manufacturing and telecommunication applications. Systems include Unisys and IBM mid range systems, file servers, LAN's, PBX systems and IBM/SNA networks.

EDUCATION: B.S., Industrial Management, 1967
              University of Texas at Austin

EXPERIENCE:

1982-Present   **Sentinel Life Insurance Company**, Boston, MA
               <u>Program Manager</u>   (1987-Present)
               Responsibilities: Manage Sentinel's forecasting and sales analysis system that incorporates advanced word processing and services for over 500 users in the actuarial, financial sales, and human resources areas. Interface directly with the user groups. Supervise a staff of three persons.
               System features: Network facilities including T-1 and special microwave, centralized control, and E-mail. Components are IBM, Northern Telecom's SL-1, Timeplex multiplexers, Codex modems, and Novell LAN's. IBM/SNA/RJE installations for branch sites, and IBM/SNA/3270 for the remote sites.
               Administrator duties: System administration, configurations, network optimization, third-party vendor evaluations, and the network users' primary interface/liaison for data processing.
               Security duties: Password updates, user ID codes and control lists, setting logical and physical attributes, and maintaining a file system protection scheme.
               Network duties: Work with ATT's nationwide network through its network manager, introduce ISDN to the Voice Communications Manager and to the use of the Northern Telecom digital PBX switch as a backbone for voice-over data integration and research new IBM PC/AT terminal emulation products for PC to host communications.

               <u>Internal Consultant</u>   (1980-1982)
               Responsibilities: initiate and produce for the following research projects dealing with actuarial rates:

EXHIBIT 5–B   Résumé (Computer Programmer): AFTER   63

Jonathan Peters (continued)

* Design and development for update system for data base tables (actuarial tables, individual insurance policy results).
* Developed corporatewide actuarial database conversion procedure to our product planners.
* Investigated techniques and systems to evaluate the data base to be maintained using real-time data.
* Instituted a system and procedures whereby we monitored system, software, and application software performance.

1976-1980   **United Telecommunications**, Kansas City, MO
Network Administrator
Responsibilities: Manage a special customer-dedicated network serving a base of 21 firms. Managed the implementation of data center, including hardware and software, procedures, telcom systems, and personnel hiring. Supervised a four-person program office.
Administrator duties: Controlled hardware and software inventories, negotiation with vendors for equipment, approving standard and extra maintenance requests.
System features: The system's nodes are IBM and Unisys. System used HDLC, X400, ASYNC, X.25, and Ethernet LANS. The system tied into Telenet, Tymnet, and international record carriers (IRC's).

1974-1976   **McDonnel Douglas,** St. Louis, MO
Operations Manager
Responsibility: Managed the firm's aircraft data base analytic system serving over 1,000 internal users and 350 aircraft user firms on an international network.

1971-1974   **Simmons, Brown and Coulter,** St. Louis, MO (40-person legal firm)
Technical specialist for a legal firm. Planned and implemented installation of special display terminals (CPT and WANG).

1967-1970   **Factorymation, Inc.,** Dallas, TX (Consulting firm in factory automation, now part of McDonnel Douglas.)
Technical Specialist/Programmer Analyst for technical support and operations of the customer service operation.

Personal   Born July 1947; married with two grown children.
Own homes in Revere and in Cape Cod; family enjoys sailing our 37' ketch on the Cape.

Member of ACM and Boston Personal Computing Society.

     EXHIBIT 5–B—Continued

Jonathan Peters (continued)

SUMMARY OF HARDWARE, SOFTWARE, AND LANGUAGES

HARDWARE:
Unisys Mid range
IBM PC/XT, PC/AT, and clones
IBM 3081K, 3084Q, 3090 200E
IBM SNA/RJE, SNA/3270 Gateways
DEC VAX 8650,8700, VAX CLUSTERS
DEC PDP-11/4.5 with special telecom mods
DEC Ethernet Controllers and Terminal Servers
MacIntosh SE and II
Timeplex Link 1 T-1 Multiplexers
Racal Milgo and Codex (modems, DEConnect)
NCR Tower
File Servers: 3COM and Banyon
Wang and CPT word processor
Communication Producer
Novell LAN

SOFTWARE:
DECNET
VAX/VMS
X.25
OS/VS2, MVS and MVS/XA
X.400
JES2, JES3
IBM SNA
MS/DOS and PC packages
Ethernet
UNIX
Oracle RDB
FFDI and Sonet specification

LANGUAGES:
ADL
COBOL
FORTRAN
C++
SAS
JCL

EXHIBIT 5–B—Continued   65

Dear Mr. Karson:

I possess an extensive set of skills in corporate operations. This has been proven by some spectacular contributions that I have made—contributions that are critical to the success of any firm.

I am certain that you would find that I possess a considerable range of talent and that I could play a key role in one of your client's firms.

Let's meet soon to discuss this.

Sincerely,

Enclosure: résumé

Do not send a cover letter like this. It serves no purpose.
It is an ineffective cover letter since it:
- Does not identify the person.
- Probably overstates the accomplishments, thereby leading to questions about the person's judgment.
- Does not use good business practice of maintaining a certain level of formality.

3 Stephen Court
Phoenix, AZ 85044
(602) 220-1175

Dear Mr. Karson:

I have been directed to your firm as being one that maintains high integrity. Due to a recent LBO that caused a cost-cutting crisis at my firm, I am currently seeking a new position. I hope that you will find my qualifications appropriate for one of your client's needs.

Specialty store management and department store operations are my areas of expertise. I have spent a number of years in two nationally known department stores achieving the position of Vice President of Operations. I have in-depth and broad experience in all aspects of sales support functions, inventory control, space analysis, budgeting, and expense control.

Since 1982, I have had the position of Vice President of Operations in a successful, rapidly expanding specialty store chain. My responsibilities also include inventory control, purchasing, support personnel, and all aspects of store growth. This also included site selection, lease negotiations, store design, and, in certain cases, construction. During my first three years in this position, my small, well-balanced management team tripled the size of the company and started a central warehousing facility, which reduced operating cost by 25 percent. We increased sales by 40 percent, increased margins by 10 percent, and lowered personnel turnover by 30 percent. We also had significant improvements in service and merchandise presentation through the implementation of a variety of innovative programs. The response from customers and employees was overwhelmingly positive.

I would appreciate the opportunity to meet a potential employer to discuss past contributions and what I could do in the future. I thank you.

Sincerely,

Donald Patrick Kelly

This is a long, detailed letter that contains words, words, words. While it all makes sense and is interesting, it does not contain anything that would catch the reader's eye—nothing to enable the reader to relate quickly to the letter or the person.

Bold italic type face may look attractive, but it is difficult to read.

3 Stephen Court
Phoenix, AZ 85044
(602) 220-1175

Dear Mr. Karson:

Due to a recent takeover of my firm, Togs R' US, I am seeking a new position as vice president of operations for a large retail operation. Prior to Togs R' US, I held similar positions at Filene's of Boston and A&S of New York. At these three firms, I reported to the EVP or COO.

Department and specialty store management operations are my areas of expertise. I have in-depth and broad experience in all aspects of sales support functions, inventory control, space analysis, budgeting and expense control—plus site selection, lease negotiations, store design, and construction.

Since 1982, I have had the position of Vice President of Operations for Togs R' US, a rapidly expanding specialty store chain based in Phoenix, serving the teenage market in the Greater Southwest region, including Southern California. Sales are $37 million. During my first three years in this position, my small, well-balanced management team *doubled* the geographic coverage of the company along with many other accomplishments.

The best was an outstanding personnel program that I set up with the Arizona Board of Education. It consisted of setting up an apprentice training program for underprivileged teenagers. Not only did it provide us with a steady stream of potential employees, it enabled us to evaluate them on the job; and by our giving them a large discount for purchasing our togs, these kids became our fashion models in the community. The response from customers and employees was overwhelmingly positive. Good business coupled with community service.

My recent base salary has been $70,000, supplemented by an excellent bonus package and perks.

I hope that you will find my qualifications appropriate for one of your clients' needs. I look forward to hearing from you in the near future.

Sincerely,

Donald Patrick Kelly

Needs "What I am".

Mathew S. Tragaskis
430 Lexington Road
Wheaton, IL 60188
(708) 868-9122

Weak résumé in content and presentation. Does not adequately present strengths and uniqueness of person.

EXPERIENCE:

MEMSCOUR GARAGE MANAGEMENT CORPORATION, Chicago, IL
General Manager/Director of Operations
1984-Present

Describe this firm. (Very interesting)

• Direct staff of 28 managers covering 40 field locations with sales of $40 million per year.

Name some locations.

• Responsible for in-house merchandising, negotiating new contracts and purchasing.

• Coordinate internal departments including legal staff, audit, bookkeeping, payroll.

Which union?

• Maintain control over all union arbitration and negotiations.

SEARS, ROEBUCK & Co., Chicago, IL
Director of Merchandising Operations—Garden Furniture
1985-1987

This is a brand name. More information is needed, however. This information can also be used to enhance person.

• Functioned as a key liaison between the Chicago office and Sears field associates (stores, distribution centers, regional offices.)

Where

• Assisted buyer in selecting product line for Sears stores.

• Negotiated pricing and delivery schedules.

Name some

• Worked with suppliers in developing new products.

• Developed strategies with marketing department for effectively merchandising Sears products.

• Supervised staff of 10 carrying out daily job functions.

TRANSAM CORPORATION, Indianapolis, IN
Manager
1973-1985

What is this firm?

• Responsible for shop floor operation

• Sales manager responsible for wholesale and retail sales function within $380,000 territory.

• Negotiate pricing and developing delivery schedules to maximize effectiveness.

EXHIBIT 8–A   Résumé (Operations Manager and Merchandising Manager): BEFORE

69

ACCOMPLISHMENTS:

Accomplishments should be related to each position. Otherwise, they lose their impact.

1989-Dissolved and successfully consolidated partially owned subsidiary into Parent company.

1988-Restructured overtime schedules resulting in a 52% cost reduction.

1988-Reduced managerial staff resulting in a 15% cost reduction.

1988-Directly responsible for generating increases of 14% after first year.

1987-Promoted three grade levels: added responsibilities from $34 million in 1986 to over $100 million in 1987.

1987-Responsible for a special buy program for West Coast Office.

1986-Responsible for 100% increase in retail sales and 50% increase in catalog sales.

1986-Minimized markdown for business unit and returned $1 million from a budget of $3.5 million.

1986-Responsible for merchandising 80,000 units (20 groups) in special buy merchandise to Sears stores.

EDUCATION:

Columbus University, Columbus, Ohio, 1975.
Bachelor of Arts, with high honors.
Management/Psychology.

Some personal information would be helpful to the reader.

Mathew S. Tragaskis
430 Lexington Road
Wheaton, IL 60188
(708) 868-9122

OVERVIEW

Director of Operations for diverse businesses (garage and properties, merchandising and inventory systems, repair facilities, etc.). Big company experience (**Sears Roebuck**) and small company experience (garage properties and auto repair). Key strengths:

- Tough, fair negotiator and respected hands-on manager.
- A problem solver who provides and implements solutions far below expected costs—and within planned time frame.
- A person who keeps management's goals as primary target.

EXPERIENCE

1984-1990 MEMSCOUR GARAGE MANAGEMENT CORPORATION, Chicago, IL
Memscour is a $40 million garage operation, managing its own garage properties and those of commercial buildings.

General Manager/Director of Operations
Directed staff of 68 managers responsible for 40 field locations (garage operations) throughout the city of Chicago, such as Wrigley Building, Chicago Museum of Art, Hyatt Hotel, and the Sears Tower.

Coordinate all in-house merchandising programs dealing with such corporations as the Hyatt Hotel and National and Avis Rent-a-Car.

Solely responsible for the research and evaluation of properties for their potential possibilities as new locations. Survey Chicago and outlying areas.

Successfully completed the opening of four new locations with a gross revenue of over $2.6 million.

Smooth personnel relationships are essential to garage operation. Developed strategies for Teamster Union negotiations and arbitrations.

Individual Accomplishments:
Defined the transition and merger plan for two independent operating companies, Mid-West Garage Management Corp. and Memscour Garage Management Corp. into one smooth operation. Operation accomplished over six months with no negative impact on output.

Reduced management staff by 16%. Reconstructed overtime schedules, resulting in a cost reduction of 52% while generating annual revenue increases of 14%.

EXHIBIT 8–B   Résumé (Operations Manager and Merchandising Manager):
AFTER

1981-1984 **SEARS, ROEBUCK & Co**, Chicago, IL   (Corporate Headquarters)

Director of Merchandising Operations—Garden Furniture
Responsible for $100 million dollars in sales. Products provided to corporate accounts, home builders, and standard consumer home garden market.
Coordinated distribution for 600 Sears Roebuck stores, 8 regional warehouses, and 10 district buying offices (Dallas, Los Angeles, Chicago, Newark, Miami, etc.).

Functioned as key liaison between Sears Roebuck and major manufacturing companies.

Worked with suppliers (Rubbermaid, Kelsey's, U.S. Furniture, Piazza Italia, and Korst of Sweden) in developing new products.

Negotiated pricing and delivery schedules.

Developed strategies with marketing department for improving merchandising campaign of the Sears Roebuck garden furniture products.

Supervised staff of 15, carrying out daily work functions.

Individual Accomplishments:
Responsible for 90% increase in retail sales and 65% increase in catalog sales.

Minimized markdown for unit and realized a return of $1,300,000 from a budget of $3,900,000.

1973-1981 **TRANSAM CORPORATION**, Indianapolis, IN
One million dollar auto machine shop operation that rebuilt and repaired manual and automatic transmissions. (Held this position while attending Columbus University.)

Manager, Reporting to President
Managed shop floor operation. Also responsible for selling activities to fleet operators. Increased gross sales from $400,000 to $1.2 million within Greater Indianapolis area.

Implemented wholesale fleet program which included such corporations as Hertz, Avis, and Budget Rent-a-Car.

EDUCATION and PERSONAL

Columbus University, Columbus, Ohio, 1981: B.A., Management/Psychology, (with high honors).
Born September, 1956; married, three teenage children; very good health.

77A Lemont Avenue
Wilmington, DE 19833
(302) 661-5477

Dear Mr. Karson:

I am currently looking for a Senior Sales or Marketing Manager position.
Some of my accomplishments are:

- Developed and implemented a reintroductory cycle for a product thought
  to be declining. This program extended the life of the product by 18
  months, thereby achieving the initial product plan's goals.

- Developed a successful strategic plan that identified and managed a
  regional presentation program, to demonstrate products at major hospital
  seminars dealing with purchasing procedures.

- Developed a plan that would concentrate on selling to residents within
  teaching hospitals (analysis showed two factors: they are the ones
  responsible for sifting through new literature, and their education is
  more oriented to high technology.)

- Led a product planning task force that defined the characteristics of a new
  state-of-the-art product.

Please feel free to contact me should you feel that my qualifications are
applicable to one of your clients. Thank you for your assistance.

Sincerely,

Raymond Woodbury

Is this a true sales letter that distinguishes this person (product) from the
thousands of other persons? It lacks many specifics such as names of firms,
industry specialty, geographic regions. This person's identity is unclear.

It would also help to indicate the salary range so the reader can immediately
perceive "how senior" this person is.

Nonbold type is better.

Weak résumé

Raymond Woodbury
77A Lemont Avenue
Wilmington, DE 19833
(302) 661-5477

Background

~~OBJECTIVE~~

A senior management position in Sales or Marketing within the health care industry. ←

Much too weak. There are thousands of people who can say this. Needs "What I am."

EXPERIENCE

1986 to Present

DUPONT CHEMICAL CO., Wilmington, DE
Hospital Products Division

<u>**Director, Western Region Commercial Operations**</u>

Many points which can be structured better.

- Coordinate activities of five regional offices whose responsibilities are to manage regional accounts, promote sales to hospitals and medical laboratories for health care systems, and maintain distributor relations. Total activity involves 90 professional sales people, systems support, and training.

- Developed and implemented a reintroductory cycle for a product thought to be declining. This program extended the life of the product by 18 months thereby achieving the initial product plan's goals.

- Identified and orchestrated a corporatewide product bundling opportunity for major hospital buying groups.

- Developed a successful strategic plan that identified and managed a regional presentation program, to demonstrate products at major hospital seminars dealing with purchasing procedures.** *Hospital Names*

Good; interesting.

- Developed a plan which would concentrate on selling to residents within teaching hospitals (analysis showed two factors: They are the ones responsible for sifting through new literature and their education is more oriented to high technology.)**

Awkward way to refer to programs.

- Introduced the two preceding programs** at corporate level. Programs adopted nationwide.

- Led a product planning task force that defined the characteristics of a new state-of-the-art product.

Product name

Avoid bold type for descriptive material.

EXHIBIT 9–B *Cover Letter/Résumé (Sales and Marketing Manager): BEFORE*

1979 to 1986   CORNING, Corning, NY
                     Hospital Products Division, Midwest Operation

Product Line Manger, Blood Gas Instrumentation Operations,
                                  1984 to 1986

- Coordinated all activities necessary for the profitable operation of the Business Unit that included a wide variety of Blood Gas Instrumentation with total sales volume exceeding $220 million; reported to the Division Vice President.

Senior Marketing Manager   1980 to 1984

- Responsible for new product introduction, collateral sales material, pricing analysis, and schedules for manufacturing and financial analysis.

- Developed list of potential third-party maintenance firms for back-up to own operation. Selected leaders based on quality of service. Developed three-year rolling forecast and annual marketing plans that defined marketing and the total activities for the product line: branch sales, expense plans, continuing R&D allocation, financial analysis (sales, margins, ROI) headquarters training, and sales collateral materials for the blood gas analysis, blood gas calibrators, and blood gas buffer products.

Marketing Manager   1978 to 1980

- Identified a new method to introduce a new model of the calibrator that produced $22 million in annual sales with a 50% margin.

1964 to 1979   BECKMAN INSTRUMENTS, Palo Alto, CA

Product Director, Multichannel Analyzer and Electrophoresis Equipment   1974 to 1978

Division Sales Manager   1972 to 1974

Field Sales Representative   1970 to 1972

Sales Representative,   1968 to 1970

Sales Representative, Supplies (paper, reagents, controls)
                                    1964 to 1968

EDUCATION   B.S. in Marketing; minor in Chemistry.
                     University of California at Davis, 1964.

Too many points. Requires better presentation.

Good. Ancient history and therefore told briefly.

More personal data. Always helpful to present full picture.

77A Lemont Avenue
Wilmington, DE 19833
(302) 661-5477

Dear Mr. Karson:

I have had senior sales and marketing positions with such firms as Dupont, Corning, and Beckman, leading their instrumentation product activities for the hospital laboratory market.

I am a leader in this field, knowing many of the key hospital groups and territories throughout the United States, the products and the people in the field. I am now seeking a position as a vice president of marketing and sales within a large firm in this field (services or products) or as a president of a modest sized firm in this market, with sales around $50 million.

Some of my recent accomplishments at Dupont are:

- Developed and implemented a reintroductory cycle for a product thought to be declining, Dupont's *ACA IIa,* extending the product's life by 18 months, thereby achieving the initial product plan's goals.

- Led a product planning task force that defined the characteristics of the new state-of-the-art *Dimension* product.

- Developed a successful strategic plan that identified and managed a regional presentation program, to demonstrate products at major hospital seminars dealing with purchasing procedures. Included Kaiser, Shriners, and California state hospitals.

- Developed a plan concentrating on selling to residents within University of California and Washington teaching hospitals.

I possess a B.S. in Marketing with a minor in chemistry, obtained at the University of California at Davis in 1964. My recent total remuneration was $75,000.

Please feel free to contact me should you feel that my qualifications are applicable to one of your clients. Thank you for your assistance.

Sincerely,

Raymond Woodbury

Raymond Woodbury
77A Lemont Avenue
Wilmington, DE 19833
(302) 661-5477

BACKGROUND

Senior sales and marketing executive with Dupont, Corning, and Beckman, leading their instrumentation product activities for the hospital laboratory market. A leader in this field, knowing the key hospitals, territories, and products. Planned new products (*Dimension*) and introduced and recycled products. Managed sales forces in the Midwest and West Coast. Seek senior sales/marketing or COO position.

EXPERIENCE

1986 to Present   **DUPONT CHEMICAL CO.,** Wilmington, DE
Hospital Products Division

Director, Western Region Commercial Operations

Management

- Coordinate activities of five regional offices (Los Angeles, Phoenix, Spokane, Denver, and Omaha) whose responsibilities are to manage regional accounts, promote sales to hospitals and medical laboratories for health care systems, and maintain distributor relations. Total activity involves 90 professional salespeople, systems support, and training.

Product Management

- Developed and implemented a reintroductory cycle for a product within the Automatic Chemical Analyzer line (ACA IIa) thought to be declining. Program extended the life by 18 months, thereby achieving the initial product plan's goals.
- Led a product planning task force that defined the new *Dimension* product.

Sales Plans

- Identified and orchestrated a corporatewide product bundling opportunity for major hospital buying groups. This included Kaiser Foundation, Shriners, and California and Colorado state hospitals.
- Developed numerous successful plans that were introduced at corporate level and adopted nationwide:
  - * Regional presentation programs to demonstrate products at major hospital seminars dealing with purchasing procedures.
  - * Concentrate on selling to residents within teaching hospitals (analysis showed two factors: they are the ones responsible for sifting through new literature, and their education is more oriented to high technology.)

Raymond Woodbury (continued)

1979 to 1986
CORNING, Corning, NY
Hospital Products Division, Midwest Operation

Product Line Manger, Blood Gas Instrumentation Operations, 1984 to 1986.
- Products included blood gas analysis, blood gas calibrators, and blood gas buffer products.
- Coordinated all activities necessary for the profitable operation of the business unit, which included a wide variety of blood gas instrumentation units with total sales volume exceeding $220 million; reported to the division vice president.

Senior Marketing Manager   1980 to 1984
- Managed new product introduction: collateral sales material, pricing analysis and schedules for manufacturing and financial analysis.
- Selected third-party maintenance firms for back-up to own operation. Selection based on quality of service.
- Developed three-year rolling forecast and annual marketing plans that defined marketing and the total activities for the product line: branch sales, expense plans, continuing R&D allocation, financial analysis (sales, margins, ROI), headquarters training and sales collateral materials.

Marketing Manager   1978 to 1980
- Identified new method to introduce a new calibrator model that produced $22 million in annual sales with a 50% margin.

1964 to 1979
BECKMAN INSTRUMENTS, Palo Alto, CA
Product Director, Multichannel Analyzer and Electrophoresis
Equipment   1974 to 1978
Division Sales Manager   1972 to 1974
Field Sales Representative   1970 to 1972
Sales Representative   1968 to 1970
Sales Representative, Supplies   1964 to 1968

EDUCATION
B.S. in Marketing, Minor in Chemistry
ROTC.
University of California at Davis, 1964.

PERSONAL
Born May 4, 1943.
Married with four grown children.
Have excellent health and enjoy outdoor sports.

EXHIBIT 9–D—Continued

James Ho
13 Carter Road
Harvey, Illinois 60426

Dear Executive Recruiter:

My firm has recently been reorganizing, and I do not see a strong path for further advancement. I am, therefore, seeking a new position that will utilize my expertise in finance and administration.

I would appreciate your reviewing and considering my background for any client assignments you may be working on. My recent title is Director of Finance, Export Operations. My base salary is $70,000.

I am submitting my résumé to you, and I do look forward to learning about an opportunity that you consider to be applicable for a person with my background.

Sincerely,

James Ho

His résumé reveals a world-class individual, someone who has made profitable corporate level deals. The cover letter should state this.

This person knows the financial instruments of foreign trade, having worked with them for many years. He also knows the trucking and steel industries. This should be stated in the cover letter.

More should be expressed in the cover letter about ties to metallurgical engineering and finance and about speaking Chinese.

EXHIBIT 10–A   Cover Letter/Résumé (Finance Manager): BEFORE   79

Good résumé. Could use better presentation to lighten appearance, such as indenting geographic examples.

James Ho
13 Carter Road
Harvey, Illinois 60426
(708) 391-4429

SUMMARY

Financial Executive with international experience with particular expertise in export financing. Possess hands-on experience in business planning and analysis, budgeting, financial controls, and treasury operations. Have demonstrated particular talent in planning and coordinating business and financial activities. Executive with extensive business experience in the Far East and fluency in Chinese (Mandarin and Cantonese).

← Can be improved with more specifics

Names of firms should be on left margin. Switch locations

BUSINESS EXPERIENCE

1984 to Present ◄──────► NAVISTAR INTERNATIONAL, Chicago, IL
A $800 million leading producer of diesel engines and heavy trucking equipment to private and government owned industries in the Far East.

Director of Finance, Export Operations *underline or bold*

Responsible for assisting the international sales organization of foreign markets by seeking and constructing financial deals that obtain a strong competitive advantage. This responsibility requires considerable liaison with domestic and foreign financing institutions. Major markets include Mainland China, Indonesia, and Thailand. Position reports to the Vice President, Finance, International. Lead the operation of a small team of specialists (eight people) responsible for funds transfer, credit policy, credit investigation, currency monitoring, and bank relations. Major accomplishments include: *too dense Make into list.*

Space = China   Entered Chinese market and achieved over $20 million in sales during the first
Indent →   year of operation with subsequent increase at the rate of 20% per year. This
           arrangement was made possible by offering special payment terms to the
           customer (representatives from the Central Government), through a creative
           system of factory and consortium of banks.

Indonesia   Developed and implemented plan to establish the firm as the main supplier of
           heavy construction equipment. This was achieved by obtaining finance in both
           Indonesia and Malaysia through local banks and private investors. Financing
           arrangements were especially favorable. *|← Indent*

Area Manager, International Finance
Responsible for treasury and credit operations for Navistar's international business. Responsibilities included the coordination of treasury activities with Navistar's foreign subsidiaries, financing activities with banking institutions, overall credit policy and implementation, customer relations, litigation supervision, and debt recovery. Major accomplishments included: *too dense Make into list*

Thailand   Negotiated a $10 million finance package that enabled the Thai Overseas
Indent →   Development Bank to act as a financing agent for Navistar's receivables from
           sales made in this country. This arrangement allowed our sales to increase from *|←*

Overseas examples are good.

James Ho (continued)

$0.45 million in 1985 to $3.6 million in 1987. The net result of this was to allow Navistar to establish itself as the premier and only supplier of such equipment in the country.

1980 - 1984   CARPENTER TECHNOLOGY, Reading, PA
A $640 million company involved in the manufacture of high quality steel and alloys for industrial purposes.

Controller, Far East
Reported directly to the President, to the vice president for finance and functionally to the CFO. Major responsibilities included the planning, analysis, and monitoring of financial activities in these areas. Conducted feasibility studies for off-shore distribution centers. Accomplishments included:

[handwritten: Space =]

Taiwan

[handwritten: Indent]

Sought out a local partner to set up joint venture to produce specialized alloy that is widely used in manufacturing of container ships produced in the Far East. Assisted in the establishment of the local joint venture and served on executive committee. The firm's sales reached $15 million during first year of operation *[handwritten: Too dense, need better presentation]* with 30% profit margins. Operation has maintained a strong record of growth. Established local company and directed its business development which resulted in the increase of local sales from $5.5 million, on export basis (1982), to $8 million (1983).

Singapore

Coordinated and designed a plan to up distribution facility in Singapore serving the Far East. The facility was funded by both U.S. and off-shore banks.
Operations in Singapore reduced U.S. overhead and shipping costs by $2 million.

1973 - 1980   CYCLOPS INDUSTRIES, Pittsburgh, PA
A $450 million company producing carbon and specialty steels through six divisions.

Supervisor, International Finance Department
Provided a variety of financial management services at International Division Headquarters and Divisional levels. Prepared economic analysis for the construction of first manufacturing plant to be located in Far East. Lived in Mainland China for two years.

Supervisor for Administration, International Operations
Responsible for the planning and coordination of administrative activities between the overseas divisions and headquarters.

EDUCATION
B.S., Accounting — University of California, San Diego (1970); minored in Metallurgical Engineering.
M.B.A., Finance — University of California, San Diego (1973).

[handwritten: Should be placed on top of résumé and/or mentioned in cover letter.]

EXHIBIT 10–B—Continued   81

James Ho
13 Carter Road
Harvey, Illinois 60426

Dear Executive Recruiter:

My firm has recently been reorganizing, and I do not see a strong path for further advancement. I am, therefore, seeking a new position that will utilize my expertise in finance and administration and my experience and background in Pacific Rim operations.

My major strength is in Pacific Rim operations. I am fluent in the Mandarin and Cantonese dialects and have a degree in accounting with a minor in metallurgy (an interest based on an old family business). Working for such firms as Navistar and Carpenter Technology, I have set up joint ventures and obtained local financing in China, Singapore, Taiwan, and Thailand. These operations have continued to prosper and grow. My associations have mainly been with diesel engines and the steel and trucking industries, but my expertise could be applied to a broad set of industries.

I would appreciate your reviewing and considering my background for any client assignments you may be working on. My recent title is Director of Finance, Export Operations. My base salary is $70,000.

I am submitting my résumé to you, and I do look forward to learning about an opportunity that you consider to be applicable for a person with my background.

Sincerely,

James Ho

EXHIBIT 10-C   Cover Letter/Résumé (Finance Manager): AFTER

James Ho
13 Carter Road
Harvey, Illinois 60426
(708) 391-4429

SUMMARY

Financial Executive with significant hands-on experience in Pacific Rim business operations. Am fluent in Chinese (Mandarin and Cantonese.) Have particular expertise in export financing. Have obtained local financing in China, Indonesia, and Singapore. Have demonstrated particular talent in planning and coordinating business and financial activities throughout this region. Established extensive business contacts in transportation, steel, and financial sectors.

BUSINESS EXPERIENCE

NAVISTAR INTERNATIONAL, Chicago, IL   **1984 to Present**

A $800 million leading producer of diesel engines and heavy trucking equipment to private and government owned industries in the Far East .

Director of Finance. Export Operations
- Responsible for assisting the international sales organization of foreign markets by seeking and constructing financial deals which obtain a strong competitive advantage. Responsibility requires considerable liaison with domestic and foreign financing institutions. Major markets include Mainland China, Indonesia, and Thailand.
- Position reports to the Vice President, Finance, International. Lead the operation of a small team of specialists (eight people) responsible for funds transfer, credit policy, credit investigation, currency monitoring, and bank relations.
- Major accomplishments include:

China   Entered Chinese market and achieved over $20 million in sales during the first year of operation with subsequent increase at the rate of 20% per year. This arrangement was made possible by offering special payment terms to the customer (representatives from the Central Government) through a creative system of factoring and consortium of banks.

Indonesia   Developed and implemented plan to establish the firm as the main supplier of heavy construction equipment. This was achieved by obtaining finance in both Indonesia and Malaysia through local banks and private investors. Financing arrangements were especially favorable.

Area Manager. International Finance
- Responsible for treasury and credit operations for Navistar's international business consisting of the coordination of treasury activities with Navistar's foreign subsidiaries, financing activities with banking institutions, overall credit policy and implementation, customer relations, litigation supervision, and debt recovery.
- Major accomplishments included:

Thailand   Negotiated a $10 million finance package that enabled the Thai Overseas Development Bank to act as a financing agent for Navistar's receivables from sales made in this country. This arrangement allowed our sales to increase from $0.45 million in 1985 to $3.6 million in 1987. The net result of this was to allow Navistar to establish itself as the premier and only supplier of such equipment in the country.

EXHIBIT 10–D   Cover Letter/Résumé (Finance Manager): AFTER   83

James Ho (continued)

CARPENTER TECHNOLOGY, Reading, PA   **1980 - 1984**

A $640 million company involved in the manufacture of high-quality steel and alloys for industrial purposes.

<u>Controller, Far East</u>
- Reported directly to the President, to the vice president for finance and functionally to the CFO. Major responsibilities included the planning, analysis, and monitoring of financial activities in these areas. Conducted feasibility studies for off-shore distribution centers.
- Accomplishments included:

Taiwan   Sought out a local partner to set up joint venture to produce specialized alloy that is widely used in manufacturing of container ships produced in the Far East. Assisted in the establishment of the local joint venture and served on executive committee. The firm's sales reached $15 million during first year of operation with 30% profit margins. Operation has maintained a strong record of growth.

                     Established local company and directed its business development which resulted in the increase of local sales from $5.5 million, on export basis (1982), to $8 million (1983).

Singapore   Coordinated and designed a plan to up distribution facility in Singapore serving the Far East. The facility was funded by both U.S. and off-shore banks. Operations in Singapore reduced U.S. overhead and shipping costs by $2 million.

CYCLOPS INDUSTRIES, Pittsburgh, PA   **1973 - 1980**

A $450 million company, producing carbon and specialty steels through six divisions.

<u>Supervisor, International Finance Department</u>
Provided financial management services at International Division Headquarters. Prepared economic analysis for the construction of first manufacturing plant to be located in Far East. Lived in Mainland China for two years.

<u>Supervisor for Administration, International Operations</u>
Planning and coordination of administrative activities between the overseas divisions and headquarters.

EDUCATION

B.S., Accounting — University of California, San Diego (1970); Minored in Metallurgical Engineering.
M.B.A., Finance — University of California, San Diego (1973).

2008 Locust Street
Philadelphia, PA 19009
September 12, 1988

Dear Mr. Karson,

Either now or in the future, you may be conducting a search for one of your clients who seeks someone with my credentials. I have enclosed my résumé for your review.

I seek a position as executive assistant to the Chief Executive or Chief Operating Officer of a large company.

I have held the position of Executive Assistant to the President (Chief Operating Officer) of Penn Central for the past four years and, prior to that, also at Penn Central, I was Special Advisor to the CFO. In this role, I was responsible for overseeing a major corporate MIS study to the stage where it was to be implemented. My compensation is $75,000.

My recognized strength is my ability to work with the top executives in the firm, keeping them informed of crucial corporate issues and operations and presenting plans and ideas to develop consensus.

My experience with other firms (including International Paper and Union Carbide) consisted of finance and administration responsibilities. Also, within the workplace and in my personal activities, I have been providing guidance on EEO programs, introduction of disabled persons into the work place, and assistance to citizens' environmental groups located in Eastern Pennsylvania and Southern New Jersey.

I can be contacted at (215) 751-6499, and I am looking forward to our discussion.

Sincerely,

Peter M. Cressup

I would leave this cover letter as it is. The position of executive assistant to a president requires that the person possess a broad set of skills in business operations and is sensitive to a wide range of issues.

EXHIBIT 11–A   Cover Letter/Résumé (Executive Assistant): BEFORE   85

PETER M. CRESSUP
2008 Locust Street
Philadelphia, PA 19009
(215) 751-6499

Good content, but presentation is too dense. Difficult to read.

SUMMARY:

Make into paragraphs.

Executive Assistant—Responsible for gathering and presenting forecasts, budgets, analyses, and technical reports. Act as facilitator among executive managers. Work with senior managers to improve their presentations. Interface with all levels of management and staff. For the COO, monitored a broad range of corporate activities, including compliance, EEO, environmental issues, human resource trends, and public attitudes.
To be able to perform this broad spectrum of duties, have experience in business planning, analytic, administration, MIS controllership, and audit functions acquired at International Paper and Union Carbide.

EXPERIENCE:

1980-Present

Make into lists. ⟶

PENN CENTRAL CORPORATION
EXECUTIVE ASSISTANT TO THE PRESIDENT 1984 to Present
Work with senior management and staff to ensure smooth management operation of the company. This covers such areas as monitoring preparation and presentation of briefings to top management, tracking the firm's involvement in environmental issues, the general tendencies of the human resource programs, including verifying that the firm is a leader in exceeding its EEO obligations. Advise the President and members of the Board on various topics, including strategic and financial planning, management development, and MIS administrative support. Formalized corporate policy program. Assessed how well the subsidiary corporations are implementing the overall directions for improving information systems and how such systems have increased the corporation's effectiveness.

Lists ⟶

SPECIAL ADVISOR TO THE CFO   1980-1984
Was responsible for coordination of study to develop a 10-year plan to restructure information systems within the firm. System enabled any newly acquired divisions to integrate with planned system. Investigated in-depth operational requirements, changing markets, expected administrative and financial procedures, government reporting requirements, and development of new reports to determine quickly the impact of any problems with divisions on the specific health of the company. Also worked with outside consulting firms.

ʳWhich ones. Name them. Excellent opportunity to introduce brand names.

All good interesting points which support position being sought.

PETER M. CRESSUP (continued)

Team completed plan in three-year period and presented results to all managers. Consensus approval. Plan was handed over to newly established position of Chief Information System Officer for implementation.

1978-1980 **NATIONAL PAPER, INC.**
FINANCIAL ANALYST
Corporate Controller's staff. Coordinated budget, capital, and long-term planning for three operating groups. Prepared monthly operating reports for Board of Directors. Prepared corporate plan to upgrade MIS systems at division and corporate levels.

1974-1978 **CARVER, CORP.**
CORPORATE FINANCIAL ANALYST
Prepared President's report to the Board of Directors. Assisted corporate SEC staff to prepare a new stock offering. Prepared a training course for top management to learn how to take advantage of features of company's MIS system.

1968-1974 **UNION CARBIDE, CHEMICAL PROCESSING DIVISION**
MANAGER OF FINANCIAL ANALYSIS   1973-1974
Member of task force to review plans for a new corporate-wide system of financial reporting. Administered preparation and presentation of division's operating and capital budget. Worked with plant managers and major U.S. government contracting agency to determine scope and size of future operation and to develop long-term plans.

ASSISTANT CONTROLLER   1972
Supervised the general accounting staff and prepared all financial reports for division and corporate management.

History; Cut down.

ASSISTANT MANAGER OF ACCOUNTING   1970-1972
Prepared monthly consolidated financial statements, operations review schedules, variance analyses, and LIFO calculations. Participated in preparation and presentation of annual budget and five-year plan.

INTERNAL AUDITOR, INTERN   1968-1970

PERSONAL Born August, 1945; married and have four grown children. Maintain a broad spectrum of personal activities related to community welfare, such as providing guidance on EEO programs, introduction of disabled persons into the work place, and assistance to citizens' environmental groups located in Eastern Pennsylvania.

Good

EXHIBIT 11–B—Continued   87

PETER M. CRESSUP
2008 Locust Street
Philadelphia, PA 19009
(215) 751-6499

SUMMARY: **Executive Assistant to the COO/CEO.**

At Penn Central Corporation, responsible for gathering and presenting forecasts, budgets, analyses, and technical reports. Act as facilitator among executive managers. Work with senior managers to improve their presentations. Interface with all levels of management and staff.

Monitor a broad range of corporate activities, including compliance, EEO, environmental issues, human resource trends, and public attitudes.

Acquired experience at International Paper and Union Carbide in business planning, analytic, administration, MIS controller-ship, and audit functions.

EDUCATION: **Boston University,** B.S., Accounting (1967).
Temple University, B.B.A., Finance (1972).
University of Massachusetts, courses in biology, chemistry and environmental issues.

EXPERIENCE:

1980-Present   **PENN CENTRAL CORPORATION**
Executive Assistant to the President   1984-Present
* Advise the President and members of the Board on various topics, including strategic and financial planning, management development, and MIS administrative support. Formalized corporate policy program.
* Work with senior management and staff to ensure smooth management operation of the company. Includes:
  1. Monitoring preparation and presentation of briefings to top management.
  2. Tracking the firm's involvement in environmental issues.
  3. Verifying that the firm is a leader in exceeding its EEO obligations.
* Assess how well the subsidiary corporations' implementations for improving information systems are increasing the corporation's overall effectiveness.

Special Advisor to the CFO   1980-1984
Responsible for coordination of study to develop a 10-year plan to restructure information systems within the firm.
* System enabled any new acquired divisions to integrate with planned system.

Peter M. Cressup (continued)

* Investigated in-depth operational requirements, changing markets expected administrative and financial procedures, government reporting requirements, and development of new reports to determine quickly the impact of any problems with divisions on the specific health of the company.
* Worked with outside consulting firms (Bain and Co. and Gartner Group).
* Team completed plan in three year period and presented results to all managers. Obtained consensus approval.
* Plan was handed over to newly established position of Chief Information System Officer for implementation.

1978-1980　**NATIONAL PAPER, INC.**
Financial Analyst
Corporate Controller's staff. Coordinated budget, capital, and long-term planning for three operating groups. Prepared monthly operating reports for Board of Directors. Prepared corporate plan to upgrade MIS systems at division and corporate levels.

1974-1978　**CARVER, CORP.**
Corporate Financial Analyst
Prepared President's report to the Board of Directors. Assisted corporate SEC staff to prepare a new stock offering. Prepared training course for top management.

1968-1974　**UNION CARBIDE, CHEMICAL PROCESSING DIVISION**
Manager of Financial Analysis　　1973-1974
Member of task force to review plans for a new corporate-wide system of financial reporting. Administered preparation and presentation of division's operating and capital budget. Worked with plant managers and major U.S. government contracting agency to determine scope and size of future operation and to develop long-term plans.
Assistant Controller　　1972
Supervised general accounting staff and prepared financial reports for corporate management.
Assistant Manager of Accounting　　1970-1972
Participated in preparation and presentation of monthly, annual budget and five-year plan.
Internal Auditor, Intern　　1968-1970

PERSONAL:　Born August, 1945; married and have four grown children. Maintain a broad spectrum of personal activities related to community welfare, such as providing guidance on EEO programs, introduction of disabled persons into the work place, and assistance to citizens' environmental groups located in Eastern Pennsylvania.

EXHIBIT 11–C—Continued　　　89

Arthur L. Wales
11722 Ridge Court
Cupertino, CA 95015
July 29, 1989

Dear Mr. Karson,

I am seeking a middle management position in the Field Support Operations of a firm that produces instrumentation for a broad range of application or one that is dedicated to the medical or genetics field. I have management experience in the instrumentation and equipment service industry. I possess both administrative and technical experience. I have enclosed my resume for your review.

My salary is in the $75K range.

If you are presently conducting a search for a person with my experience, I would appreciate the opportunity to discuss the position with you. I would consider a position on the West Coast or in the Southwest. I look forward to a continuing association.

Sincerely,

Arthur L. Wales

Fair cover letter which can be improved by including these points from résumé:
* Has been in field for about 20 years and presently has a managerial title. Could show key features of background.
* Has worked for Hewlett Packard and Beckman Instruments—both brand name firms.
* Has B.S. degree from U.C.L.A. with specialties in communications, writing, and chemistry (to show good communications skills combined with a technical background).

EXHIBIT 12–A   Cover Letter/Résumé (Manager, Field Support Operations): BEFORE

With exception of 'objective', résumé is good. [Use of 'bold' for overall dates with a firm clearly shows time with each firm]

Arthur L. Wales
11722 Ridge Court
Cupertino, CA 95015
(408) 213-6941

OBJECTIVE

Product planning manager/product support manager within customer service operation for an instrumentation or medical electronics firm.

Poor. Needs a strong 'What I am'.

SUMMARY

Significant management experience in the instrumentation equipment services industry:

- Provide product planning/feature analysis for all new products to facilitate maintainability.
- Supported subsidiaries and distributors from corporate operations by providing technical and administrative guidance and support.
- Provided the international sections with product support plans.
- Facilitated U.S.-wide, special industry sectorwide, and international sales and support of products.
- Initially established a worldwide system of depots for quick reaction spare parts inventory—and later reorganized system to utilize overnight package mail services.
- Analyzed the costs associated with equipment reliability, maintainability, and service operations.

EXPERIENCE

HEWLETT-PACKARD INSTRUMENTATION DIVISION, FIELD SUPPORT OPERATIONS, 1979 - Present

Product Planning Manager for Field Support Issues   1987-Present

Provide feature analysis for all new products to facilitate maintainability and reliability. This includes telecommunication facilities built into the instruments to enable support centers to monitor and detect faults.

This item was done long time ago. Do not include. Present only current events.

To whom does this position report? Need to show level in firm.

Field Support Operations Manager, Western Hemisphere Operations   1985-1987

Served as the prime interface between U.S. based operations and South American, Latin American, and Canadian distributors for product marketing activities and for implementing product support plans.

Name Key Latin American Countries.

Facilitated hemispheric sales of product and service contracts to distributors and end-users. Coordinated training, spare parts policies, and equipment installation schedules; monitored the site performance of the specific equipment and service organization centers.

Analyzed and monitored organizational, technical, and administrative problems through liaison with customers, corporate headquarters' organizations, and field offices. Designed and implemented an on-line call-in system, reporting all equipment problem areas.

Field Engineering International Product Manager   1982-1985

Recognized that previously installed depot system was too expensive and that firm could take advantage of reliable overnight package delivery firms on worldwide basis, and thus overhauled depot system and instituted to contracts with delivery firms.

Good. This is interesting. Might be expanded upon.

Wrote a departmental phase-out plan for certain parts of the worldwide depot system. This involved restructuring personnel assignments and dealing with local distributors.

Monitored the implementation of customer service and distributor service strategies abroad. Coordinated all field changes and retrofit activity for the international areas. *Where?*

Field Engineering Account Mgr., Northern Europe   1981-1982

Provided technical/logistical/administrative support to the distributors' major customers in Northern Europe. *Name countries.*

Manager, Spare Parts Depot Planning and Operations   1979-1981

Developed a plan to increase effectiveness of customer support operations by installing worldwide key spare parts depots. Plan covered eight centers in Europe, North Africa, and Far East.

VLSI TECHNOLOGIES, 1975-1979
Product Support Analyst

Evaluated customer specifications for customized integrated circuits. Provided technical and administrative support to outside sales representatives. Managed the order-entry department.

BECKMAN INSTRUMENTS, CUSTOMER SERVICES DIVISION, 1970-1975
Assistant Supervisor   1972-1975

Managed the U.S.-wide service activities of the firm's service operations to all health-affiliated organizations. This included private and not-for-profit hospitals, military installations, special clinics and medical research organizations.

History. Could be shortened or deleted.

Analyst, Reliability Analysis Department   1970-1972
Analyzed and reported on the costs, cost-effectiveness of the firm's various reliability programs, and the impact of failure rates, maintainability, and service costs on each product line's profit and loss.

EDUCATION

B.S. , U.C.L.A., 1969; majored in Communications, Writing, and Chemistry.

PERSONAL

Married; have three children, ages 10, 15, and 18.
Born January, 1948; health: excellent.

Arthur L. Wales
11722 Ridge Court
Cupertino, CA 95015

Dear Mr. Karson:

I am seeking a middle management position in the Field Support Operations of a firm that produces instrumentation for a broad range of applications or one that is dedicated to the medical or genetics field. I have 20 years' management experience working for industry leaders, Beckman Instruments and Hewlett-Packard.

Based upon my strong insights into maintenance operations, I am currently Product Planning Manager for field support issues and am a member of Hewlett-Packard's Reliability Council. Other key parts of my background include:

- Managed Western Hemisphere field support operations for HP's instrumentation division.
- Planned and established worldwide depot system and integrated this with overnight package delivery systems to provide quick-reaction maintenance support.
- Have provided leadership within the firm in providing close support to company and distributor operations on a worldwide basis.
- Have managed a 10 person operation.

I have a B.S. in communications, writing, and chemistry from U.C.L.A

My salary is in the $75K range. I would consider a position on the West Coast or in the Southwest. I look forward to hearing from you in the near future.

Sincerely,

Arthur L. Wales

Arthur L. Wales
11722 Ridge Court
Cupertino, CA 95015
(408) 213-6941

OVERVIEW

A Product Planning and Product Support manager, *Customer Service Operations*
in the instrumentation field, with 20 years' experience. Worked for **Hewlett-Packard** and
Beckman Instruments. Planned and implemented support systems on a worldwide
basis. Direct contacts in the EEC, Japan, and South America. Understand all the critical
aspects of product support, including equipment features, logistic support, and distributor
relationships. Managed teams of 10 people.

Significant contributions in the instrumentation equipment services industry during past 10
years:

- Provide product planning/feature analysis for all new instrumentation
  products to facilitate maintainability.
- Member of Hewlett Packard's Reliability Council
- Supported subsidiaries and distributors from corporate operations by
  providing technical and administrative guidance and support.
- Provided the international sections with complete product support
  plans.
- Facilitated U.S.-wide special industry sectorwide and international sales
  and support of products.
- Initially established a worldwide system of depots for quick-reaction
  spare parts inventory—and later reorganized system to utilize overnight
  package mail services.

EXPERIENCE

HEWLETT-PACKARD   **1979-Present**
INSTRUMENTATION DIVISION, FIELD SUPPORT OPERATIONS,

Product Planning Manager for Field Support, 1987-Present
Provide feature analysis for all new products to facilitate maintainability and reliability. This includes telecommunication facilities built into the instruments to enable
support centers to monitor and detect faults. Work with hardware and software
engineers and manufacturing groups. Team reports to vice-president of
marketing.

Field Support Operations Manager, Western Hemisphere Operations, 1985-1987
Served as the prime interface between U.S. based operations and South and
Latin American and Canadian distributors for product marketing activities and for
implementing product support plans. Managed a team of 10 professionals.
Made annual visits to Sao Paulo, Mexico City, and Toronto. Reported to the
director of worldwide field support operations.

Facilitated hemispheric sales of product and service contracts to distributors and
end-users. Coordinated training, spare parts policies, and equipment installation
schedules; monitored the site performance of the specific equipment and service organization centers.

EXHIBIT 12–D   *Cover Letter/Résumé (Manager, Field Support Operations):*
AFTER

Arthur L. Wales (continued)

Analyzed and monitored organizational, technical, and administrative problems through liaison with customers, corporate headquarters' organizations, and field offices. Designed and implemented an on-line call-in system, reporting all equipment problem areas.

Field Engineering International Product Manager, 1982-1985
Major International Reorganization Activity
* Recognized that previously installed depot system was too expensive and that firm could take advantage of reliable overnight package delivery firms on world-wide basis. Overhauled depot system and instituted to contracts with delivery firms including DHL and Flying Tigers.
* Prepared a departmental phase-out plan for certain parts of the world-wide depot system. This involved restructuring personnel assignments and dealing with local distributors. Participated in resolution of major labor issues in Italy and Spain.

Monitored the implementation of customer service and distributor service strategies abroad. Coordinated all field changes and retrofit activity for the international areas with specific emphasis on the EEC and Japan.

Field Engineering Account Mgr., Northern Europe, 1981-1982
Provided technical/logistical/administrative support to the distributors' major customers in Northern Europe. Visited with distributor and company operations in Denmark, Sweden, Finland, and Northern Germany.

Manager, Spare Parts Depot Planning and Operations, 1979-1981
Developed a plan to increase effectiveness of customer support operations by installing world-wide key spare parts depots. Plan covered eight centers in Europe, North Africa, and Far East.

VLSI TECHNOLOGIES   **1975-1979**

Product Support Analyst for customized integrated circuits.

BECKMAN INSTRUMENTS, CUSTOMER SERVICES DIVISION   **1970-1975**

Assistant Supervisor, U.S.-wide service activities, 1972-1975

Analyst, Reliability Analysis Department, 1970-1972

EDUCATION

B.S., U.C.L.A., 1969; majored in Communications Writing and Chemistry.

PERSONAL

Married; have wife and three children, ages 10, 15, and 18
Born January, 1948; Health: excellent.

EXHIBIT 12–D—Continued   95

Mr. X

PROFESSIONAL GOAL

Product sales support, systems support, turnaround, and dynamically growing firm, where dynamic management, technical know-how and attention to getting the facts right are applied to building teams of excellence, producing market-winning products and capturing and maintaining a happy and growing customer base—the stockholders, bonuses to the key contributors—and a healthy growth situation.

PROFESSIONAL SUMMARY

With more than 25 years of responsible executive experience in marketing, system development, planning, and implementation of major materials handling and inventory systems. Systems consisted of computer systems, terminals, computer software, stacker cranes, system unit controllers, bin storage systems, local site transportation systems including monorail and security systems, system procedures, hiring procedures, training, subcontracting, and dealing with vendor companies.

ABILITIES

A natural leader who communicates well with superiors, coworkers and members of my team through oral and written means...a tireless worker who works with the big picture and the overall goals of the firm, while at the same time, giving strictest attention to detail. . .a broad conceptualizer. . . a strategist and an implementer. . . proposal preparation. . . customer presentations. . . project turnaround. . . team builder. . . administrator. . . financial controls. . . sets the big picture priorities. . . contract negotiator. . . subcontractor and supplier evaluation project plans. . . monitors milestones. . .understands the technology, people and the environment.

(The rest of the résumé.)

#13 shows only the introduction to a résumé. It is representative of the introductions to some of the résumés I receive. The introduction lacks focus and a true definition of what the person is. It is too wide-ranging in goals, experience and abilities. It is not a serious presentation.

I suggest the writer learn how to present himself or herself.

While we are on the subject of introductions to résumés, it might be helpful to review other introductions that are unacceptable so that your résumé does not contain introductions such as these. They all lack brand names and they consist of meaningless words.

SUMMARY: Experienced project manager with proven and successful general and program management skills covering diverse environments and all phases of product development, including project management, operational and program planning, using CAD development tools and techniques, sales and customer support, proposal preparation and marketing, staff development and contract negotiation.

OBJECTIVE: To take the lead role in developing and instituting a management framework for the 1990s that enables a financial institution that is a service–driven operation to become a healthy, dynamically growing, *Fortune 500*–contender business.

BACKGROUND: More than 15 years of dynamic and successful executive experience in general management, business planning and development, product planning and systems development and implementation, leadership, finance, sales and marketing, team management, personnel development, and manufacturing/engineering.

OBJECTIVE: To obtain a senior management position with a dynamic, future–minded firm where my background in the agribusiness world and general business management, coupled with my M.B.A., can make a significant long–term contribution toward success.

OBJECTIVE: With five years' experience in operations driving force behind the growth of one of the country's best known providers of leadership, management and product development programs, and specialized system support services, I seek a new challenge in a facility service organization, or in a facility service operation in a large company, as executive vice president, director of operations or executive director.

OBJECTIVE/SUMMARY: COO of a medium–sized company or division of a large company. Experienced manager with over 20 years of progressive responsibility. Significant accomplishments in the areas of:

Turnaround Situations	Operations
Start ups	Human Resource Development
Sales Growth	Product Planning
Market Development	Strategic Planning

Michael Zandal
18-12 Route 3
Dayton, OH 45395
Home (513) 662 1232

Dear Mr. Karson:

Your firm has a reputation for quality work. So do I! Therefore, I believe we should work together. I would like to tell you a few things about myself.

In 1982, I took on my first president's position. Since that time, I have had the challenge to turn around two companies from losers to winners. Towler Paper Goods, a family-owned paper products company with sales of $130 million was draining the family of all its accumulated wealth. They were thinking of selling it for a song. Referred to the Towler family by their local bank, I joined the firm as president with a modest salary, but a very significant bonus. In one year, we stopped hemorrhaging. In just under two years, results were profitability and a strong cash flow. The bank, the family, and I were very happy.

Heartland Express, a superior regional delivery company (sales $25 million), handling everything from letters to light machinery, is specifically dedicated to serving the industrial heartland (Ohio, Indiana, Illinois, and Western Pennsylvania). The owners invited me in and gave me three years to expand operations by 120 percent—all with internal financing. Three short-haul aircraft, four helicopters, 20 vans. Only 22 months later, we attained all our objectives, resulting in another contented group of owners.

The owner's financial position has changed since October 1987. Heartland Express is only a part of their investments, and we are short of cash to enable the expansion I want and need for my own increase in equity. We have plenty of cash for operations and no bank debt.

Now that I have proven my ability to perform turnarounds and grow firms, I want to head a small to medium company (up to $75 million) where the owners make a commitment to investing in the firm at a rate that matches the growth I will be making in revenue and profits; and my remuneration is to be closely linked to my performance.

Call me when you have time to learn more about me. The best time is in the evening after 8P.M. or during the weekend.

Sincerely,

Michael Zandal

Even though this letter is not accompanied by a résumé, I like it. It shows the person's relaxed style and his ability to work in both product and service industries, and it tells a lot about the person.

This letter can be made more formal and can also indicate the person's management style. A more formal version of this letter can be sent to the owners of firms that the person is interested in running.

Mr. Simon McFarland, Chairman
Bisway Corporation
300 Charlotte Drive
Dover, NJ 07801

Dear Mr. McFarland:

I have recently decided to leave my position as president and general manager of a profitable regional delivery company (sales $25 million). If you contact the owners of that firm or of my previous firm, I am sure that they will attest to my abilities to manage and grow a firm.

I am writing to you since I have selected Bisway from a survey I made of firms in Western New Jersey that are privately owned and ones that I felt would be interested in a person with my talents and experience. This letter will provide you with some insight into my abilities, and I plan to telephone your office next week to provide any additional information you may wish. Perhaps we can also discuss a meeting.

In 1982, I took on my first president's position. This was with Towler Paper Goods of Paterson, NJ, a family-owned paper products company with sales of $45 million. The firm was draining the family of its accumulated wealth, and they were thinking of selling it for a ridiculously low price. I was referred to the Towler family by their local bank, and I joined the firm as president with a modest salary, but a very significant bonus. In one year, we stopped hemorrhaging. In just under two years, results were profitability and a strong cash flow. The bank, the family, and I were very happy.

I left Towler in 1987 since they did sell the firm—for a far better price than they ever thought they could get. I had an important role in arranging the sale. I joined Heartland Express, a superior regional delivery company (sales $25 million) that handles everything from letters to light machinery and is specifically dedicated to serving the industrial heartland (Ohio, Indiana, Illinois, and Western Pennsylvania). The owners invited me in and gave me three years to expand operations by 120 percent—all with internal financing. An operation consisting of three short-haul aircraft, four helicopters, and 20 vans—and many people I personally trained.. Only 22 months later, we attained all our objectives. I met all operational and financial plans.

We have plenty of cash for operations and no bank debt but the owners' financial position has changed dramatically since October 1987. Heartland Express is only a part of their investments, and we lack the cash to make the planned expansion.

Now that I have proven my ability to perform turnarounds and grow firms, I want to head a small to medium company (up to $75 million), where the owners would make a commitment to investing in the firm at a rate that matches the growth I expect to be making in revenue and profits. I also wish that my remuneration be closely linked to my performance.

Concerning my management style, I enjoy working for private owners, and their interests are always paramount. I am a hands-on, walk-the-floor, go-out-to-meet-the-people manager. I like people and develop excellent, loyal teams at all levels.

I look forward to discussing our respective plans during my call next week.

Sincerely,

Michael Zandal

EXHIBIT 14–B   *Letter without Accompanying Résumé: AFTER*   **99**

Marcia Gallager

6102 Porter Drive   Minneapolis, MN 55416   (612) 342-6691

Dear Mr. Karson:

I have attached my résumé for your review. I have been successful in my career at both Digital Equipment Corporation and Data General, and my marketing experience provides a suitable background for a career with a competitor organization or with a major user organization. My computer business background is supplemented by sales management (1976-1982) in a family owned business, specializing in the manufacturing of fabrics.

I would be pleased if you would call me to discuss opportunities which you believe would be applicable to a person with my background. I prefer that you contact me at my home number or, if urgent, at my office on (612) 631-2424. I appreciate discretion in this matter.

I look forward to hearing from you in the near future.

Very truly yours,

Marcia Gallager

Letter is ineffective. It puts this person into a group with thousands of others. It lacks singularity and neglects to give the idea of any product specialty and industry specialty or to give the level of the person.

This person has a B.S. from the University of Chicago, a brand name school. This should be cited in the cover letter.

Do not use italic type.

**EXHIBIT 15–A   Cover Letter/Résumé (Computer Sales/Marketing Manager):
BEFORE**

Marcia Gallager

6102 Porter Drive   Minneapolis, MN 55416   (612) 342-6691

[handwritten: A vague résumé. Could represent anyone, selling in any industry.]

Objective: A position for a strong sales or marketing manager who knows the minicomputer business and how systems are used in the customer environment.

PROFESSIONAL EXPERIENCE

[handwritten: Needs "What I am".]

DIGITAL EQUIPMENT CORPORATION   (3/85 - Present)

AREA MARKETING MANAGER, St. Paul, MN (3/87- Present)
Responsible for all aspects of strategy development pertaining to the marketing of DEC mainframe hardware and software throughout the state. Implemented local product introduction programs.

[handwritten: Manages how many people?]

Major Accomplishments:

[handwritten, left margin: All are bland. Must make more interesting]

*Overall business volume responsibility for over $210 million sales.

*Implementation of specific competitive strategies with the marketing teams resulting in a 95% winning percentage.

*Participation in special consultant organization seminars that were funded by DEC user organization.

*Establishment of executive briefings, including seminars for more than 250 customers.

*Personnel and career development responsibility for the area's marketing team.   *[handwritten: Name some.]*

*Responsibility for sales/expense forecasts.

[handwritten: Name some products to provide brand names.]

MARKETING MANAGER, Chicago, IL   (11/85 - 3/87)
Directed a sales force responsible for the marketing of the entire DEC product line—hardware, software, and services across a *Fortune 50* corporation's major international affiliates.

Major Accomplishments: *[handwritten: How many people?]*

[handwritten, right: If names of customers cannot be mentioned, cite industry.]

*Management and implementation of a worldwide marketing plan including the setting of personnel and skill requirements to support the customer.

*Extensive contact with customer executives to ensure affiliate satisfaction and to align DEC's marketing activities with the customer's business objectives.

*Personnel and career development responsibility for the marketing team.

*Responsibility for sales/expense forecasts to management.   *[handwritten: Repetitive]*

*Yearly quota of over $80 million. Achievement of 120% of business objectives in 1987. Recipient of a branch management award in 1987 for leadership and sales experience.

EXHIBIT 15–B   Cover Letter/Résumé (Computer Sales/Marketing Manager): BEFORE

DATA GENERAL CORPORATION (3/81 - 11/85)
    BRANCH MANAGER, Des Moines, IO (11/85 - 383)

*Responsibility for the entire DG product line. *[handwritten: Sounds pompous. It would be better to cite some of the better-known products.]*

*Branch sales were $29 million.

*Responsibility for sales/expense forecasts.

*Personnel and career development responsibility for the branch's sales teams.

*Branch consistently overachieved goals in all years and was annually awarded special achievement citations.

[handwritten: Repetitive. If included, make interesting.]

ACCOUNT MARKETING REPRESENTATIVE, Des Moines, IO (3/82 - 11/85)
National Account Manager for a *Fortune 250* customer and marketing representative to two large divisions of *Fortune 150* companies. Responsible for the sale of the entire DG product line. *[handwritten: Name of firm or type of industry.]*

Major Accomplishments: *[handwritten: Sounds pompous]*

*Achieved sales of complete set of minicomputer line and application software for office automation (CEO system), distribution, and telecommunications systems. *[handwritten: Good]*

*Participated at industry symposia and seminars such as the regional Joint Computer Conferences and Comdex.

*Consistently overachieved goals in all years and was annually awarded special achievement citations.

FROSTMAN FABRICS (9/76 - 3/81)

VICE PRESIDENT SALES, Chicago, IL
A family business, sales $2 million. Business was sold in 1982 to a British wool firm and the new owner put in its own management team.

EDUCATION

THE UNIVERSITY OF CHICAGO. *[handwritten: Place at beginning]*
B.S. in Economics, 1976, with major in Marketing and minor in Statistics.
Honors included Dean's List and and membership in two honorary societies.

INTERESTS

Theater, tennis, and all water sports.

PERSONAL

Born July 1955; married with two children; own home; excellent health.

6102 Porter Drive

Marcia Gallager
Minneapolis, MN 55416

(612) 342-6691

Dear Mr. Karson:

I am currently a marketing manager at Digital Equipment Corporation, having the responsibility for the introduction and marketing support of the corporation's broad range of products throughout the state of Minnesota. I presently manage 20 people, and I have had both sales and marketing positions (within Digital and with Data General) concentrating in the northern part of the Midwest. I have handled such important accounts as the Federal Reserve of Chicago, LaSalle National, Cargill, and United and Northwest Airlines.

My business background in the computer industry is supplemented by my executive sales responsibilities (1976-1982) in a family-owned business, specializing in the manufacturing of fabrics. I possess a B.S. in Economics from the University of Chicago (1976).

My recent remuneration has been $75,000 plus incentive bonuses ranging at 15 percent.

I would be pleased if you would call me to discuss opportunities that you believe would be applicable to a person with my sales and marketing background. I wish to remain in information system sales and marketing, encompassing computers, telecommunications, and application software.

I prefer that you contact me at my home number or, if urgent, at my office (612) 631-2424. I appreciate discretion in this matter.

I look forward to hearing from you in the near future.

Very truly yours,

Marcia Gallager

6102 Porter Drive	Minneapolis, MN 55416	(612) 342-6691

OVERVIEW

Marketing and Sales manager in the minicomputer business who has worked for DEC and Data General and has concentrated in the northern part of the Midwest. Managed major accounts in the region's financial, commodity, and transportation industries (Cargill, United and Northwest Airlines, the state government of Minnesota and a *Fortune 50* manufacturer of heavy-duty power and transportations systems). Have consistently overachieved goals in all years and have been awarded annual special achievement citations.

EDUCATION

THE UNIVERSITY OF CHICAGO
B.S. in Economics, 1976, with major in Marketing and minor in Statistics. Dean's List and and two honorary societies.

PROFESSIONAL EXPERIENCE

DIGITAL EQUIPMENT CORPORATION   **3/85 - Present**

AREA MARKETING MANAGER, St. Paul, MN   (3/87- Present)
Responsible for marketing strategy for DEC mainframe hardware and software throughout the state. Implement local product introduction programs, manage team presentations to 25 key accounts such as Cargill, Northwest Airlines, governor's office, state treasury, and motor vehicle divisions. Marketing unit responsible for over $210 million annual revenue, managing over 100 important accounts. Manage 20 professionals.
Major Accomplishments:
* Implemented specific competitive strategies with the marketing teams, resulting in a 95% winning percentage.
* Participated in over 40 special consultant and VAR organization seminars that were funded by DEC user organization.
* Established executive briefings, including seminars for more than 250 potential customers including Minnetonka Corporation and Federated Mutual Insurance Company.
* Developed personnel and career development programs keyed specifically to the background and culture of Minnesota, including courses on the state government and the finance and business infrastructure of the state, ethics in the sales and workplace, treatment of coworker disabilities and drug problems.

EXHIBIT 15–D   Cover Letter/Résumé (Computer Sales/Marketing Manager): AFTER

MARKETING MANAGER, Chicago, IL   (11/85 - 3/87)
Direct a sales force responsible for the marketing of the DEC product line (hard-ware, software, and services) across a *Fortune 50* corporation's major interna-tional affiliates. This corporation is a leader providing heavy-duty power and transport systems. Its markets and spare parts depots are worldwide.
* Managed and implemented a worldwide marketing plan including the setting of personnel and skill requirements.
* In addition to weekly contacts with MIS directors, met with corpo-rate MIS executives quarterly to provide status report on present orders to DEC.
* Monitored any changes from the corporation's projected buying plans.
* Informed MIS executives of new products and any problems DEC may be facing in product deliveries.
* Met with CEO annually, along with senior vice president of DEC to provide DEC corporate overview and to learn of DEC's perceived performance.
* Had yearly quota of over $80 million. Achieved 120% of business objectives in 1987. Received a branch management award in 1987 for leadership and sales experience.

DATA GENERAL CORPORATION   **3/81 - 11/85**

BRANCH MANAGER, Des Moines, IO   (11/85 - 383)
* Had branch sales of $29 million.
* Sold complete set of minicomputer line and application software for office automation (CEO system), distribution, and telecommuni-cations systems.
* Started career participation at industry symposia and seminars such as the regional Joint Computer Conferences and Comdex.
* Responsible for sales/expense forecasts.
* Responsible for personnel and career development for the branch's sales teams.

ACCOUNT MARKETING REPRESENTATIVE, Des Moines, IO (3/82 - 11/85)
National Account Manager for a *Fortune 250* customer (agribusiness) and market-ing representative to two large divisions of *Fortune 150* company (aircraft parts).

FROSTMAN FABRICS   **9/76 - 3/81**

VICE PRESIDENT, SALES, Chicago, IL
A family business, sales $2 million. Business was sold in 1982 to a British wool firm, and the new owner put in its own management team.

PERSONAL
Born July 1955; Married with two children; own home; excellent health.
INTERESTS
Theater, tennis, traveling, and camping in family's recreational vehicle.

EXHIBIT 15–D—Continued   105

Robert L. Flannery
1131 Anderson Avenue
Chicago, IL 60652

Dear Mr. Karson:

I have recently decided to seek out a new position and I am writing to you to make you aware of my job search. I have enclosed my résumé for your review.

My goal is a Chief Information Officer position or other significant corporate role that will allow me to utilize my experience and skills. My strengths lie in understanding the techniques involved in information system development, project management and problem solving. I'm a person who seeks challenges. I am a high-energy person. While most of my experience has been in manufacturing, I believe that it can be applied across a broad spectrum of business, including financial and service operations.

I would appreciate your contacting me for any situation in which you consider I would be an appropriate candidate. You may call me at home (312) 886-9797 or office (312) 621-1390. At the latter location, discretion is requested.

Sincerely,

Robert L. Flannery

This letter is typical of those that I receive from managers of MIS. But it is representative of many of the letters I receive from other functional areas such as human resources, purchasing or manufacturing. Such letters typically lack distinction or singularity.

They can be improved in many ways to make them brand name résumés, such as showing involvement with non-MIS issues. That is, these letters (and résumés) should show involvement and concern with the firm's overall health.

EXHIBIT 16–A   Cover Letter (Management Information System Manager): BEFORE

Robert L. Flannery
1131 Anderson Avenue
Chicago, IL 60652

Dear Mr. Karson:

I am writing to you to make you aware of my job search. I am presently the vice president for management information systems for a moderate-sized ($50 million) manufacturing firm. We manufacture automotive replacement parts, specializing in the mid-range Japanese import cars such as Toyota and Nissan. This necessitates the maintenance and control of a diverse and expensive inventory. The MIS function is the key to a profitable operation.

We maintain this on a VAX-NCR hybrid system that supports terminals in our customers' distribution offices, performing inventory control, data capture, shop floor control and monitoring, as well supporting CAD/CAM systems. I took over this activity when it was run on a simple IBM 360/30 batch system.

Since that time, I have built an MIS department that is responsive to both internal and customer needs. For example, my managers and I meet frequently with our own shop floor supervisors and the firm's customers to be abreast of their needs. We attend industry conferences, both for users and for developers, so that we can assess properly how and when we should be improving our system.

Through my leadership, the team is aware that its mission is to promote a smooth operation in all areas of the firm and to increase profitability. My managers and I attend all interdepartment operational meetings—marketing and sales, finance, human resources, and manufacturing—providing the core for intracompany communication.

I am a member of the company's executive committee, consisting of the CEO, the CFO, and the vice president of manufacturing. Most issues dealing with customer relations and IS are within my purview. My most recent salary was $80,000 supplemented by the opportunity for a 20 percent incentive bonus.

If you know of a firm that seeks a high energy person with a comprehensive understanding of MIS and how it impacts on P&L, please call me.

Sincerely,

Robert L. Flannery

An Open Letter to Human Resource Professionals

Your profession has probably the most far-ranging and sensitive role in a firm, covering hiring and personnel policies, personnel standards, selection of key people, and evaluating staffing levels. You are also called upon to deal with an evolving set of social issues that the firm and the community face, such as the plight of the homeless, drugs and AIDS. You are also called upon to resolve a wealth of individual and corporate-level problems such as CEO succession. Given this many-faceted role, the head person in human resources may well be the *éminence grise* in the firm. Your résumés, however, frequently do not show clearly these diverse and important responsibilities and contributions.

To show your uniqueness and far-ranging contributions, I suggest that you group your accomplishments into categories, such as shown below. I also suggest that you stress the more timely issues that you have worked on, possibly reducing your coverage of standard issues.

A good HR résumé should always indicate the size of the firm in which you exercised your profession, in terms of dollar sales or number of employees and number of overseas operations or branches under your purview.

I have listed some of the varied contributions that HR people are responsible for. There are many more that could be listed. The purpose of this list is to show that by defining the category of the contribution, you will present a stronger, more focused résumé.

Personnel Installed companywide human resource review system for talent identification and development. Similarly, established demotion plan that received union approval.

Established and staffed affiliate company in Mexico and regional sales offices in Honduras and Costa Rica, including recruitment, selection, and training of 50 local national managerial and professional employees.

Created a vision of what acquired and developing businesses should be like organizationally and introduced employee programs and support systems to reinforce desired work cultures.

Managed multiple executive searches ($110K-$280K) and successfully restaffed, within nine months the top-management team reporting to the COO.

Corporate Provided counsel to Board of Directors, CEO, and Staff on organization, manpower, and human resources issues.

Was a member of five-person team (COO, CFO, EVP operations, and Chief Legal Officer) to plan reorganizations, acquisitions, and dispositions.

Profitability Even though the firm operates within a government-regulated area, set up "profit culture" courses to show employees that their adopting a "competition mentality" will provide them with personnel and financial benefits.

Instituted a salary/contribution evaluation program aimed at correcting inequities in management compensation. Resulted in increased profitability through many avenues: increased management effectiveness, decreased turnover and loss of noncontributing managers. Established regional Human Resources network, resulting in 50 percent reduction in Human Resources travel budget.

Establish HR The firm had been acquiring and disposing of firms at the rate of two per year without any corporate HR policy to guide and transform diverse operation and cultures. Established Corporate Human Resources Function. Maintained company control at unit level but provided key policies resulting in decreased personnel turnover (average 8 percent) throughout the firm.

Succession Set up a succession plan for all positions from senior vice president to CEO.

Upon the request of the chairman, developed a plan to make the abrupt transition to the new president from the incumbent president. Had one week to prepare plan and did changeover in five days, starting with announcement to key managers (Friday night). Introduction and management meeting with new president (over weekend) and announcements with firm (Monday) to customers, financial community, and vendors (Monday and Thursday).

Union Issues Won NLRB representation elections with increasingly comfortable margins.

Negotiated union contracts with two unions (the Teamsters and the IEU) as spokesman for company. Settlements were timely, peaceful, and within budget.

Shut-down During a recent downsize from 50 thousand to 40 thousand employees and the closing of two plants, set up a broad spectrum of programs to minimize rumors and assist people in relocating or finding new positions in community: hot line, special editions of firm's newsletter, daily open forums held after working hours; assistance for short term loans, and outplacement programs.

Takeover Firm was taken over by a foreign firm that requested that we change certain well-established management procedures. Headed a task force which set up plan to phase in certain changes while showing parent firm the potential cultural problems associated with a few of the procedures. Received approval to delete the latter group.

Social Issues Established special service group and 24-hour assistance hot line to assist personnel with acute and immediate problems (drugs, family squabbles, family accidents, health, etc.).

Established corporate policies on dealing with drug situations, such as detecting drugs in candidates and among employees, support meetings, education programs, and family support.

Provided consulting on crucial social issues to diverse divisions that are part of the corporation: immigrant labor, drugs, and alcohol.

Community Local community received large influx of Cambodian immigrants, which placed burden on community services. Defined corporation's community assistance program and internal education program.

Maintained high community profile for the company through service on Board of Directors of Opera, President of Chamber Orchestra Board, and service on United Way committees.

EXHIBIT 17—Continued   109

Arnold Cane
90 4th Avenue
New Brunswick, NJ 08899
(201) 527-8976

A Management Executive ← *What is this* *Words, Words, Words.*

with strong skills in manufacturing, administration, and finance. Am considered an expert in operations and turnarounds. I possess a B.S. in Industrial Engineering and an M.B.A. A solid track record of success in turning losing operations into effective, positive cash-flow operations, providing sound management controls in rapidly growing environments. Have been involved in all phases of business operations. A skilled, team-building executive with superb communication skills. I have shown leadership qualities to management and have been an integral part of the top management team.

Sounds like everyone

CAREER HIGHLIGHTS

This is a list of recent career highlights! Say so.

- Defined and implemented a cost-saving program that turned a loss-ridden company into a profitable operation.
- Changed fundamental business policies and practices—controls, credits receivables, inventory control, organization, and administration.
- Defined tight cost controls and buying practices that vastly improved an off-shore operation with estimated savings of $22 million per year.
- Set up new ways to decrease receivables significantly, winning favor of bank by extending line of credit.

PROFESSIONAL EXPERIENCE

Good résumé from here on down.

RAYTRAN CONCRETE CORPORATION, 1985 to Present

Director of Administration and Finance
Led the turnaround of a company on the verge of bankruptcy. Brought in new team of strong middle-level financial manager and a top controller, stopped high-roller operations, evaluated overhead costs throughout firm, and reorganized administrative and finance operations. Made firm profitable with strong positive cash flow.

- Introduced "just-in-time" inventory techniques, eliminating $100,000 in finance costs and increasing inventory turnover.

- Cut down administrative organizational staff by 30%, with minimal—but acceptable—loss in productivity. Introduced tight travel and expense controls that had been nonexistent in past.

- Showed marketing organization how to evaluate contribution to profit of distribution and sales organization. Enabled them to separate losers from winners and to stick only with winners.

Prefer two pages. Cut down or use smaller type.

EXHIBIT 18–A   Résumé (Business Manager, Administration and Finance): BEFORE

- Set up new financial reporting system that closely watched ROI, cash flow and receivables, thereby winning bank's favor with larger credit line.

THE RYLAND GROUP, 1982 to 1985

Director of Controls
Established systems, procedures, and internal controls for this $1.2 billion construction and selling firm, which specializes in single family homes.

- Improved cash flow by reducing receivables to 100 from 200 days and accelerating billing cycles to better reflect project status.

- Instituted new job site hiring practices, which reduced personnel turnover to 6% from 16%

- Established corporate policies covering limits of authority, organization reporting schemes, and established audit function for field operation.

- Restructured purchasing department, implemented new procedures and controls, and eliminated conflicts of interest between purchasing and inventory management.

Good

DUPONT CORPORATION, 1971 to 1981

Plant Financial Controller, Building Supply Products, 1976 to 1981
Analyzed product cost structure for the division in manufacturing facilities throughout the U.S. and U.K., which ultimately led to the closing of three manufacturing plants that were not profitable. Developed a reporting system that showed profitability of each operation. System enabled expansion and contraction of facilities according to individual contribution.

- Revised reporting methods on scrapped material effecting $11 million savings throughout facilities.

- Established department standards for management and EDP auditing. Instituted formal project control techniques.

- Changed plant maintainance procedures (introduced preventive maintenance) resulting in 22% increase in up-time of production system.

Good

Regional Audit Manager, Southeast Region, 1971 to 1976
- Managed audit and analysis of the division's operations. Conducted reviews of plant operations and regional headquarters operations.

- Conducted detailed analytical review of total factory operations, EDP and networking support operations, buying procedures, and personnel policies.

EXHIBIT 18–A—Continued   111

My high standard of performance was recognized by management, leading to my being designated to controller for the entire building supplies product line manufacturing operation in the U.S. and the U.K.

Good

BLACK AND DECKER (A $5 billion quickly growing leader in power tools), 1966 to 1971

Auditor, Team Leader, 1967 to 1971

History.
Can be
cut down.

- Analyzed and prepared operational audit reports on the U.S. manufacturing facilities.

- Instrumental in changing the receivable and payable policy which resulted in an 8% decrease in bank credit needs. Recommended 4% increase in pricing with no negative impact on customer preference for the products.

Manager, Product Cost Control, 1966 to 1967

Managed and coordinated budgets, costs, and controls for the design and prototype departments.

EDUCATION AND RELATED PROFESSIONAL ACTIVITIES

Education: M.B.A., Finance/Marketing, University of Maryland, 1967.
B.S. Industrial Engineering, University of Pennsylvania, 1965.

Professional
Organizations: American Society of Industrial Engineers.
American Management Association.

Personal information

Arnold Cane
90 4th Avenue
New Brunswick, NJ 08899
(201) 527-8976

SUMMARY

Financial and administration executive with expertise in controlling and cutting costs in all aspects of a company's operation—manufacturing, administration (travel, factory overhead, receivables, etc.), and personnel. Have worked in large, stable firms (**Dupont, Black and Decker, and the Ryland Group**) as well as a firm I helped pull back from the brink of bankruptcy (Raytran Concrete). Specific expertise in building supply and construction industries. I work as an outstanding contributor to the executive team. Have excellent personal reputation in industry, which enables me to attract new team members.

EDUCATION

M.B.A., Finance/Marketing, University of Maryland, 1967.
B.S., Industrial Engineering, University of Pennsylvania, 1965.

RECENT CAREER HIGHLIGHTS—A TURNAROUND

- Defined and implemented a cost-saving program that helped turn a loss-ridden company into a profitable operation.

- Changed fundamental business policies and practices—controls, credits receivables, inventory control, organization, and administration.

- Defined tight cost controls and buying practices, which vastly improved an off-shore operation with estimated savings of $22 million per year.

- Set up new ways (MIS controls, new reporting systems, dunning task force) to decrease receivables significantly, winning favor of bank by extending line of credit.

PROFESSIONAL EXPERIENCE

RAYTRAN CONCRETE CORPORATION, New Brunswick, NJ   1985 - Present
Raytran is a privately held $110 million firm providing building materials to the commercial construction industry. It serves the Northern New Jersey and New York City markets.

Director of Administration and Finance
Led the turnaround of a company on the verge of bankruptcy. Brought in new team of strong middle-level financial managers and a top controller, stopped high-roller operations, evaluated overhead costs throughout firm, and reorganized administrative and finance operations. Made firm profitable with strong, positive cash flow.
- Introduced "just-in-time" inventory techniques, eliminating $100,000 in finance costs and increased inventory turnover.
- Cut down administrative organizational staff by 30%, with minimal—but acceptable— loss in productivity. Introduced tight travel and expense controls that had been non-existent in past.
- Showed marketing organization how to evaluate contribution to profit of distribution and sales organization. Enabled them to separate losers from winners, and to stick only with winners.
- Set up new financial reporting system that closely watched ROI, cash flow and receivables, thereby winning bank's (MidLantic) favor with larger credit line.

Arnold Cane (continued)

THE RYLAND GROUP, St. Louis, MO   **1982 - 1985**

Director of Controls
Established systems, procedures, and internal controls for this $1.2 billion construction and selling firm, which specializes in single family homes.

- Improved cash flow by reducing receivables to 100 from 200 days and accelerating billing cycles to better reflect project status.
- Instituted new job site hiring practices, which reduced personnel turnover to 6% from 16%
- Established corporate policies covering limits of authority, organization reporting schemes, and established audit function for field operation.
- Restructured purchasing department, implemented new procedures and controls and eliminated conflicts of interest between purchasing and inventory management.

DUPONT CORPORATION, Wilmington, DE   **1971 - 1981**

Plant Financial Controller, Building Supply Products   1976 - 1981
Analyzed product cost structure for the division in manufacturing facilities throughout the U.S. and U.K. which ultimately led to the closing of three manufacturing plants that were not profitable. Developed a reporting system that showed profitability of each operation. System enabled expansion and contraction of facilities according to individual contribution.

- Revised reporting methods on scrapped material effecting $11 million savings throughout facilities.
- Established department standards for management and EDP auditing. Instituted formal project control techniques.
- Changed plant maintainance procedures (introduced preventive maintenance) resulting in 22% increase in up-time of production system.

Regional Audit Manager, Southeast Region   1971 - 1976
- Managed audit and analysis of the division's operations. Conducted reviews of plant operations and regional headquarters operations.
- Conducted detailed analytical review of total factory operations, EDP and networking support operations, buying procedures, and personnel policies.

My high standard of performance was recognized by management, leading to my being designated controller for the entire building supplies product line manufacturing operation in the U.S. and the U.K.

BLACK AND DECKER, Baltimore, MD   **1966-1971**
A $5 billion quickly growing leader in power tools.

Auditor, Team Leader   1967 - 1971

Manager, Product Cost Control   1966 - 1967

PROFESSIONAL ORGANIZATIONS

American Society of Industrial Engineers.
American Management Association.

Robert Gregg
99 Babcock Place
Huntsville, AL 35844

Dear Mr. Karson:

I am seeking a senior financial position with a growing organization where my leadership and experience can contribute to bottom-line results.

Some of the features of my background are:

- Saved $6 million annually by redefining a JIT operation.

- Directed and implemented a three-year plan, which turned around a manufacturing firm from a $2.5 million loss to $500,000 profit in two years.

- Increased sales (200%) and cash flow (25%) in the first year through a change in receivable and payable policies, introduction of a new vendor evaluation program, revision to pricing, commission structure, and incentive program for sales people.

- Accelerated shipments to customers through changes in the order entry system.

My current compensation is $85,000 plus an expected bonus of $15,000. My home phone number is (205) 303-7864.

Sincerely yours,

Robert Gregg

This letter lacks brand names and is bland. It shows no intrinsic abilities that would help the reader learn more about the person.

The letter lists features that show the person has done more than finance. This ability to contribute to other domains in the firm should be clearly cited.

EXHIBIT 19–A   Cover Letter/Résumé (CFO): BEFORE   115

Robert Gregg
99 Babcock Place
Huntsville, AL 35844
205 303-7864

Good overall résumé

But needs a brand name and "What I am". This is too wordy. Not specific. Words, words, words. Sounds like anyone who is a 'financial executive.'

BACKGROUND

Senior Financial Executive with 18 years of industry experience in both financial controls and financial management with special emphasis on systems and implementation. A business person mentality who knows how to evaluate and work with the varied operational units such as sales and marketing, operations, administration, and human resources. Implemented turnaround in a medium-sized manufacturing company. Focused on RIO and profitability. People-oriented with team-building, motivational skills.

KEY ACCOMPLISHMENTS

1988 to Present **SESLEY WIRING COMPANY, Division of Penn Central Corporation**
CFO and Director, Administration

To show COO abilities in a clearer way, these features on accomplishments should be shown according to category, such as finance, HR, manufacturing.

- Directed the design of a three-year rolling forecast/business plan that encompassed:
  . Product line evaluations
  . Market analyses and projections
  . Vendor analysis
  . Resource planning (funds, personnel, equipment and materials)
  . Plant locations
  . Information systems

- Revitalized sales and marketing by formulating a new pricing policy structure, commission plan, and incentive program and analyzed the vendor's contribution.

- Changed receivable and payable policies, increasing cash flow by 25%.

- Introduced "just-in-time" relationships that shortened manufacturing lead times to 6 months from 8 months.

- Developed corporate policy statements for HR department which changed corporate culture and reduced personnel turnover.

- Enabled $1.5 million reduction in inventory through introduction of new MRP II system.

1984 to 1988 **MAYNES MANUFACTURING COMPANY**
Vice President, Finance

- Managed 50 person finance department.

- As Executive Committee member, managed, consolidated, and relocated the manufacturing operation to Taiwan facility with an annual savings of $22 million.

- Evaluated U.S. manufacturing facilities and determined which three should be closed.

Good page

- Developed an MIS system for Taiwan facility, allowing it to be responsive to both long term and sometimes disruptive short-term product needs of the corporation.

- Instituted system for operational audits across all business operations, identified five potential hot spots in first year.

- Defined the method for shipping products between manufacturing facility and home plant systems integration facility.

1981 to 1984 **COMBUSTION ENGINEERING, Corporate Operation**
Assistant Controller

Supervised 160 people, responsible for monitoring financial operation of entire corporation.

1973 to 1981 **COMBUSTION ENGINEERING PROCESS AUTOMATION BUSINESS DIVISION**
Manager, Division Accounting Services

A software systems firm that added to CE's capability to do reactor monitoring.

1969 to 1973 **UNITED TECHNOLOGIES, Pratt & Whitney Division**
Senior Financial Analyst 1972-1973
Financial Analyst 1969-1972

- Managed multimillion dollar parts inventory for jet engines located at airports throughout the country.

- Member of team that initiated several new contracts with major airlines purchasing Pratt & Whitney aircraft engines.

EDUCATION

B.S., University of Bridgeport, Bridgeport, CT, 1968.

EXHIBIT 19–B—Continued   117

Robert Gregg
99 Babcock Place
Huntsville, AL 35844

Dear Mr. Karson:

I am a financial executive with almost 20 years' experience, concentrating my activities in large manufacturing and industrial firms such as Sesley Wiring, a division of Penn Central, Combustion Engineering, and Pratt & Whitney of United Technologies. While my contributions have been mainly in finance, I have also worked with the corporation's other executives to provide guidance and direction in their respective areas.

Having performed much in the same way as a COO, I believe I have two job options: A large firm could be interested in me as an EVP/CFO, or a modest-sized one (up to $200 million) would consider me for COO. To indicate my contributions in both financial and nonfinancial matters, I cite a group of recent accomplishments performed at Sesley Wiring Company:

COO functions
Manufacturing

- Enabled $1.5 million reduction in inventory through introduction of new MRP II system.
- Introduced "just-in-time" relationships which shortened manufacturing lead times to six months from eight months.

Sales

- Revitalized sales and marketing by formulating a new pricing policy structure, commission plan and incentive program.

Human Resources

- Developed corporate policy statements for the HR department that changed corporate culture and reduced personnel turnover.

CFO function

- Directed the design of a three-year rolling forecast and business plan that encompassed:
  . Product line evaluations
  . Market analyses and projections
  . Vendor analysis
  . Resource planning (funds, personnel, equipment and materials)
  . Plant locations
  . Information systems
- Changed receivable and payable policies, increasing cash flow by 25%.

My compensation is $100,000 plus an expected bonus of $15,000. When you have an opportunity that is applicable to my background, I would appreciate your contacting me.

Sincerely,

Robert Gregg
99 Babcock Place
Huntsville, AL 35844
205 303-7864

OVERVIEW

Senior Financial Executive with strong COO skills. Have demonstrated ability to manage and lead both financial and a full business operation. Believe that both strong financial and operational audits are the responsibility of the CFO. Have received excellent management training at **United Technologies** and **Combustion Engineering**. Seek CFO position at major industrial or COO at mid-sized firm.

EXPERIENCE

1988 to Present

SESLEY WIRING COMPANY, Division of Penn Central Corporation
Sales are $250 million. Provides electrical wire to the U.S. manufacturers of civilian aircraft and military aircraft.

CFO and Director for Administration

Finance
- Directed the design of a three year rolling forecast/business plan that encompassed:
  Product line evaluations
  Market analyses and projections
  Vendor analysis
  Resource planning (funds, personnel, equipment and materials)
  Plant locations
  Information Systems
- Changed receivable and payable policies, increasing cash flow by 25%.

Manufacturing
- Enabled $1.5 million reduction in inventory through introduction of new MRP II system.
- Suggested to vice president manufacturing that I seek services of Connecticut-based consulting firm, Manu-Systems, to audit study potential impact of a JIT system. Study's recommendation implemented and new "just-in-time" system, which shortened manufacturing lead times to six months from eight months.

HR
- Initiated operational audit of personnel turnover, identifying need for better awareness of corporate actions and policies among hourly employees.
- Developed corporate policy statements for HR department that changed corporate culture and reduced personnel turnover.

Sales
- Revitalized a moribund sales and marketing operation by formulating a new pricing policy structure, commission plan, and incentive program. Suggested new pricing policies to Sesley's defense industry customers (Boeing, Rockwell, McDonnel Douglas, etc.) increasing sales to that sector by 42%.

EXHIBIT 19–D   Cover Letter/Résumé (CFO): AFTER   119

1984 to 1988	**MAYNES MANUFACTURING COMPANY** Sales are $180 million. Manufacturing of high-production but high quality plastic and metal furniture for the commercial markets (hotels, airline terminals, movie theaters, stadiums, concert halls, etc.)

Vice President, Finance

- Managed 50-person finance department.

- As Executive Committee member, managed, consolidated, and relocated the manufacturing operation to Taiwan facility with an annual savings of $22 million.

- Evaluated U.S. manufacturing facilities and determined which three should be closed.

- Developed an MIS system for Taiwan facility, allowing it to be responsive to both long term and sometimes disruptive short term product needs of the corporation.

- Instituted system for operational audits across all business operations, identify five potential hot spots in first year.

- Defined the method for shipping products between manufacturing facility and home plant systems integration facility.

1981 to 1984	**COMBUSTION ENGINEERING, Corporate Operations** Sales are $3.5 billion. A worldwide company providing energy systems, both fossil and nuclear fuels.

Assistant Controller
Supervised 160 people and was responsible for monitoring financial operation of entire corporation.

1973 to 1981	**COMBUSTION ENGINEERING, Process Automation Division** Division was established to supplement CE's standard product line of energy systems by providing a full-service operation of feasibility studies, design, turnkey implementation, training, and facility operation.

Manager, Division Accounting Services

1969 to 1973	**UNITED TECHNOLOGIES, Pratt & Whitney Division**	
	Senior Financial Analyst	1972-1973
	Financial Analyst	1969-1972

- Analyzed multimillion dollar parts inventory for jet engines located at airports throughout the country.
- Member of team that initiated new contracts with major airlines purchasing Pratt & Whitney aircraft engines.

EDUCATION

B.S., University of Bridgeport, Bridgeport, CT, 1968.

EXHIBIT 19–D—Continued

Mitchel Haussman, Ph.D.
6335 Park Way
Kingsport, TN 37665
(615) 338-1995

Dear Mr. Karson:

I presently have a very responsible position, but potential for professional growth is limited due to cutbacks in corporate R&D funds. Therefore, I am considering a career move in search of greater professional challenge as a director of research and development within the plastics industry.

The enclosed résumé highlights my career accomplishments. You will note that I have been involved in managing R&D teams in fundamental and applied research for major corporations. I have a reputation for developing products that have medium term commercial success and for assisting the marketing staff in its commercialization of the ultimate products.

I would appreciate the opportunity to discuss my career objectives with you so you can better present my credentials to your clients. I look forward to hearing from you.

Sincerely,

```
Key brand name items missing from cover letter are firms, examples of some
R&D leading to products, and university degree.
```

EXHIBIT 20–A   Cover Letter (Director, R&D): BEFORE   121

Mitchel Haussman, Ph.D.
6335 Park Way
Kingsport, TN 37665
(615) 338-1995

Dear Mr. Karson,

I presently have a very responsible position at Eastman Kodak's Eastman Chemical Division, but potential for professional growth is limited due to cutbacks in corporate R&D funds. I am, therefore, considering a career move in search of greater professional growth and challenge within the plastics industry. Fields of particular interest include polyallomer/polybutylene and polypropylene plastics.

Since graduating from Rennselaer Polytechnic Institute in 1960 with a Ph.D. in Chemistry, I have worked for two leaders in the field, Dow Chemicals and Eastman. For the past 10 years, I have concentrated on directing projects that meet the growing issues of environmental protection and industrial waste. To demonstrate this, I changed the direction at Dow Chemical from thermoset (nonrecyclable) to degradable substances.

I have a reputation for developing products that have medium-term commercial success and for assisting the marketing staff in its commercialization of the products.
I am presently managing four project teams with an annual budget of $1.6 million.

My salary this past year has been $100K plus an incentive bonus of 30 percent, which I have successfully obtained for the past three years. Relocation is not a problem for my family of four, which consists of my wife and our two teenage children.

I would appreciate the opportunity to discuss my career objectives with you so you can better present my credentials to your clients. I look forward to hearing from you.

Sincerely,

Mitchel Haussman, Ph.D.

EXHIBIT 20–B   Cover Letter (Director, R&D): AFTER

267 Maiden Lane
Appleton, WI 54911

Dear Recruiter:

A recent LBO, coupled with a merger of my firm with another firm controlled by the investors, has forced me to search for a new career opportunity. My primary interest is in the chemical production industry as a Chief Financial Officer for a major firm or as a COO for a modest sized firm ($50 to $100 million.)

I have enclosed my résumé for your review in hopes that you may be interested in someone with my background and experience. The following are some of my special accomplishments:

- Over 20 years of experience managing all operations of corporate finance.

- Significant experience in the chemical industry.

- Skills in strategic planning, acquisitions of new facilities integration and spawning of corporate divisions, and financial restructuring.

- Direct technology experience backed up by a technical education.

- Significant concern and guidance with corporate HR role.

- Extensive experience in MIS, administration functions.

- First hand experience working in Europe.

Please do not hesitate to call me at (414) 869-0217 should you have further interest in my background.

Very truly yours,

Steven R. Berk

Mr. Berk can strengthen a few areas of accomplishments, according to the list on the résumé. He has been associated with brand name firms in European locations and should cite these. He has an M.B.A. and a B.S. in Chemical Engineering, which should also be cited in the cover letter.

EXHIBIT 21–A   Cover Letter/Résumé (Financial Officer or COO): BEFORE   123

STEVEN R. BERK
267 Maiden Lane
Appleton, WI 54911
(414) 829-0217

Good content

Could be improved by better "What I am."

PROFESSIONAL OBJECTIVE:

Senior management position with responsibilities over finance, control, planning, and administration. Primary interest is in a high growth opportunity specializing in the chemical industry.

EXPERIENCE:

4/85 - Present **Wyamote Process Systems**   Appleton, WI
EXECUTIVE VICE PRESIDENT AND CHIEF FINANCIAL OFFICER

Wyamote Process System is a manufacturer of equipment for use by the chemical processing industry. Operations include five manufacturing sites with annual sales of $200 million and 2,100 employees. *← Where?*
Responsible for all administrative functions, which include finance, planning, corporate and plant MIS operations, and human resources. Plant controllers report on a dotted line. Supervise a staff of 105 people.

Good

Achievements:

* Planned and participated in major restructuring activities that included site closures and acquisitions. Due to this restructuring, company profits have improved more than 25% in the last two years following a four-year decline.

* Modernized and expanded the MIS functions. Implemented a connection to an international network enabling daily activity reports to be available at headquarters. MRP II system and converting all major financial subsystems.

* Negotiated a difficult labor agreement that modified the employee benefits package by focusing on expanding and previously uncontrollable health care costs.

Good points

* Set up a study team to examine potential impact on firm due to revisions expected in EEC in 1992.

* Suggested to vice president of human resources ways to decrease losses due to drug users within plants.

5/79 - 3/85   **ICI, Inc.**   Houston, TX, and London, United Kingdom
CORPORATE CONTROLLER AND CHIEF FINANCIAL OFFICER

ICI is England's leading company in the chemical industry with various subsidiary operations in the U.S. In 1980, it initiated a joint venture with Exxon, conducting research relating to chemical processing.

Good

Responsible for the initiation of the finance function and managed control, treasury, tax, and construction planning of the joint venture. Was a member of management committee and supervised 80 people. Acted as Chief Financial Officer for the joint operation and served on the Executive Finance Committee for the U.S. corporate headquarters.

The general format could be improved by widening right and left margins. Provides a "lighter" appearance

Achievements:

* Involved in all aspects of a company start up: site selection, recruiting, construction, product definition, definition of reports to parent companies.

* Participated in raising $200 million in new capital in various forms of financing that included equity, long term loans provided by a consortium of local banks plus working capital financing.

2/78 - 2/79   **DuPont Corp., International Plastics Division,** The Hague, Netherlands
GROUP FINANCIAL PLANNING MANAGER
Responsible for operational and financial planning for a major DuPont plastic international operation in the production and distribution areas with sales of $400 million.

Achievements:

* Implemented new planning systems and procedures and participated in reorganization efforts that improved profits.
* Directed and managed cost cutting program and plant overhaul, resulting in a 22% increase in sales.

6/73 - 2/78   **DuPont Corp.,** Wilmington, DE
FINANCIAL MANAGER

Initially hired as a financial analyst; subsequently promoted to Financial Manager of the International Plastics Division with sales of over $1.3 billion.

Achievements:

* Generated savings in Delaware site by redefining the way raw materials would be shipped to the plants and initiated the restructuring of assembly operations.
* Analyzed accounting and management information flow in overseas plastic subsidiaries and suggested new reporting methods. Introduced new methods facilitating a 17% reduction in financial reporting, staff requirements, reducing each subsidiary staff. (Staff reduction was achieved by imposing a hiring freeze.)

10/69 - 5/73   **U.S. Steel,** Pittsburgh, PA
SYSTEMS ANALYST

Designed and installed computer systems for control and financial applications, personnel files, inventory and ledgers. [Promoted the idea of seeking outside application software packages through software vendors or through other firms that may have developed systems for similar problems.]

[handwritten: History. can be deleted.]

EDUCATION: *[handwritten: ← Put at beginning. Name brands and directly applicable to career.]*

M.B.A., Major: Finance, University of Pittsburgh, 1971.
B.S., Chemical Engineering, Specialty in Metallurgy, University of Pittsburgh, 1969.

PERSONAL:
Born 10/10/46; married; wife, Pamela; two children, Vincent and Harold; excellent health.

COMMENTS: *[handwritten: Not appropriate. Leave out.]*

My major strength is the ability to translate complex technical and operational issues into clearly defined financial models enabling all persons involved in the decision process to understand the situation in all its dimensions. *[handwritten: Put up front.]*

EXHIBIT 21–B—Continued   125

267 Maiden Lane
Appleton, WI 54911
(414) 869-0217

Dear Recruiter:

A recent LBO, coupled with a merger of my firm with another firm controlled by the investors, has forced me to search for a new career opportunity. I have held general management and CFO positions in the chemical production industry, working for such firms as ICI and DuPont. I have provided executive leadership in all key issue areas, both financial and nonfinancial, such as coping with foreign competition, reassigning operational responsibilities due to the tough foreign competition, and the drug problem.

I now seek a position as CFO for a major firm or as a COO for a modest sized firm ($50-$100 million.).

The following are some of my special accomplishments:

- Over 20 years of experience managing corporate finance operations within the chemical industry.

- Skills of a COO in strategic planning, acquisitions of new facilities, integration and spawning of corporate divisions, operations, and financial restructuring.

- Significant concern and guidance with the corporate HR role and facing the realities of the work place, such as coping with the drug problem.

- Extensive experience in MIS and administration functions, starting from my earlier work with U.S. Steel.

- Firsthand experience working in Europe, in the U.K. and the Netherlands, plus planning studies to assess impact on U.S. operations by EEC's 1992 changes.

I am known by my colleagues to have the natural ability to translate complex technical and operational issues into clearly defined financial models, enabling all persons involved in the decision process to understand the situation in all its dimensions.

I also bring to bear strong industry-related academic credentials, having a B.S. in Chemical Engineering and an M.B.A. in Finance, both from the University of Pittsburgh. My recent remuneration was $135,000, supplemented by significant perks.

Should you have further interest in my background, please do not hesitate to call me at home during the evening or on the weekend.

Very truly yours,

Steven R. Berk

STEVEN R. BERK

| 267 Maiden Lane | Appleton, WI 54911 | (414) 829-0217 |

OVERVIEW

General Manager and CFO in the chemical production industry, working for such firms as ICI and DuPont. Provide executive leadership in all key issue areas, both financial and nonfinancial, such as coping with foreign competition, reassigning operations due to the tough foreign competition, and the drug problem. Now seek a position as CFO for a major firm or as a COO for a modest-sized firm ($50 to $100 million).

Major strength is the ability to translate complex technical and operational issues into clearly defined financial models, enabling all persons involved in the decision process to understand the situation in all its dimensions.

EDUCATION

M.B.A., Major: Finance, University of Pittsburgh, 1971
B.S., Chemical Engineering, Major in Metallurgy, University of Pittsburgh, 1969

EXPERIENCE

4/85 - Present **Wyamote Process Systems,** Appleton, WI
Executive Vice-President and Chief Financial Officer
Wyamote Process System is a manufacturer of equipment for use by the chemical processing industry. Operations include five manufacturing sites with annual sales of $200 million and 2,100 employees. Two of the facilities are located in Northern Italy.
Responsible for all administrative functions, which include finance, planning, corporate and plant MIS operations and human resources. Plant controllers report on a dotted line. Supervise a staff of 105 people.

Achievements
* Planned and participated in major restructuring activities that included site closures and acquisitions. Due to this restructuring, company profits have improved more than 25% in last two years following a four-year decline.
* Modernized and expanded the MIS functions. Implemented a connection to an international network enabling daily activity reports to be available at headquarters. MRP II system and converting all major financial subsystems.
* Negotiated a difficult labor agreement that modified the employee benefits package by focusing on expanding and previously uncontrollable health care costs.
* Set up a study team to examine potential impact on firm due to revisions expected in EEC in 1992.
* Suggested to vice president of human resources ways to decrease losses due to drug users within plants.

5/79 - 3/85 **ICI, Inc.,** Houston, TX, and London, United Kingdom
Corporate Controller and CFO
ICI is England's leading company in the chemical industry with many subsidiary operations in the U.S. In 1980, it initiated a joint venture with Exxon, conducting research relating to chemical processing.

EXHIBIT 21–D   *Cover Letter/Resumé (Financial Officer or COO): AFTER*   127

Responsible for the initiation of the finance function and managed control, treasury, tax, and construction planning of the joint venture. Member of management committee and supervised eighty people. Acted as Chief Financial Officer for the joint operation and served on the Executive Finance Committee for the U.S. corporate headquarters.

Achievements
* Involved in all aspects of a company startup: site selection, recruiting, construction, product definition, definition of reports to parent companies.
* Participated in raising $200 million in new capital in various forms of financing that included equity, long term loans provided by a consortium of local banks plus working capital financing.

2/78 - 2/79 **DuPont Corp., International Plastics Division,** The Hague, Netherlands
Group Financial Planning Manager
Responsible for operational and financial planning for a major DuPont plastic international operation in the production and distribution areas with sales of $400 million.

Achievements
* Implemented new planning systems and procedures and participated in reorganization efforts that improved profits.
* Directed and managed cost-cutting program and plant overhaul resulting in a 22% increase in sales.

6/73 - 2/78 **DuPont Corp.,** Wilmington, DE
Financial Manager
Initially hired as a financial analyst, subsequently promoted to Financial Manager of the International Plastics Division with sales of over $1.3 billion.

Achievements
* Generated savings in Delaware site by redefining the way raw materials would be shipped to the plants and initiated the restructuring of assembly operations.
* Analyzed accounting and management information flow in overseas plastic subsidiaries and suggested new reporting methods. Introduced new methods facilitating a 17% reduction in financial reporting and staff requirements. (Staff reduction was achieved by imposing a hiring freeze.)

10/69 - 5/73 **U.S. Steel,** Pittsburgh, PA
Systems Analyst
Designed and installed computer systems for control and financial applications, personnel files, inventory, and ledgers.

PERSONAL
Born 10/10/46; married; two children; excellent health.
Supplement my business travel with extensive family and personal travel to Europe and the Far East, enabling me to understand cultural patterns and how they relate to business operations.

Richard (Dick) Collins
626 Horton Avenue
Dayton, OH 45411
(513) 880-2445

Dear Mr. Karson:

I am seeking a position as President or General Manager of a manufacturing company. My area of expertise is managing businesses in competitive markets. I would also consider another turnaround situation.

I have had true general management responsibility for the past 10 years. These positions covered complete profit and loss responsibility, as well as total sales, manufacturing, marketing, and financial accountability.

As you can see in my résumé, I was originally with large firms where I learned techniques that I have since applied to the smaller operation that I ran. I am a humanistic executive who thrives on teams and developing people. I know what is going on in my operation by "walking the factory floor." I am also a results-oriented, tough-minded manager who has successfully met turnaround challenges and demonstrated ability to maximize profit and enhance growth—all with a growing ROI.

My current compensation is in the low six-figure range, and I would be willing to relocate for the right position.

I would be pleased to hear from you.

Yours truly,

Richard (Dick) Collins

While parts of the cover letter are good, most of it has ineffective wording. What kind of manufacturing company and products has he been involved with? Letter should indicate *some* special abilities in the areas of finance, the manufacturing process, sales, or training.

It would be appropriate to indicate the size of the firms in terms of sales.

Nicknames: Show either the nickname Dick <u>or</u> the proper name Richard, not both.

No nicknames ↓

Richard (Dick) Collins
626 Horton Avenue
Dayton, OH 45411
(513) 880-2445

Words, words, words.
Need specifics.

SUMMARY:

An executive in manufacturing firms who has managed both growth and turn-around situations in diverse products lines. A general manager who can transform losers to winners. A bottom-line oriented executive who is responsive to the people he works with. Have been Division General Manager of successful turnaround situations, transforming non-profitable organizations into profitable ones. History of significant accomplishments in cost control and in creating a humanistic environment in metal industry. Bring experience in manufacturing, sales and products serving consumer and industrial markets in both made-to-order and high volume products.

PROFESSIONAL EXPERIENCE:

Highlight → firms' names throughout.

BRACE-IT, Dayton, OH   1987 to Present
Manufacturer and distributor of specialized steel and aluminum bracing products to strengthen walls, floors, and ceilings in overloaded buildings.
<u>Executive Vice President and General Manager</u>
Responsible for aluminum products' profit and loss performance. Accountabilities include marketing, finance, manufacturing, design, research and development, and quality assurance. In first year, shut down 20% of product lines, increasing profits by 24%. Other accomplishments:

Many points should be listed by category, such as finance, Sales, HR.

- Repositioned product lines.
- Developed and launched new products for commercial and residential market segments.
- Introduced training courses for first time in history of firm. (Enabled firm to reduce new hiring program, reducing direct and overhead staffs by 16%.)
- Introduced five-year rolling forecast into firm.
- Changed local banks and obtained improved financing arrangements.

OKTAL ALUMINUM, Dayton, OH   1986 to 1987
Manufacturer of specialized aluminum products selling to manufacturers of factory floor equipment (conveyers, inventory, etc.)
<u>Executive Vice President</u>
Chief Operating Officer of multiplant operation, responsible for total profit and loss performance. Some accomplishments:

- Developed and implemented three year rolling forecast for capital and operational requirements.
- Increased total order backlog 75%.
- Reduced break-even point 25%.
- Achieved quality assurance levels of 99% and serviceability rate of 95%.

EXHIBIT 22–B   Cover Letter/Résumé (General Manager of Manufacturing Company): BEFORE

- Instituted new catalog system, decreasing reliance on local distributors.
- Called for new hiring procedures to enable better evaluation of candidates.

SPENCER PLATFORMS, Pittsburgh, PA   1980 to 1986
Manufacturer and distributor of special flooring equipment for factory floors.
<u>Vice President and General Manager</u>
Responsible for total division profit and loss performance. Other accomplishments:
- In first year, made firm profitable after previous two years of loss.
- Restructured sales force by setting up regional operation to allow direct sales people to be closer to customer.
- Achieved 25% ROI.
- Selected and implemented new MIS operation.

MEXLER INDUSTRIES, Indianapolis, IN   1977 to 1980
Manufacturer and distributor of high quality aluminum fasteners and braces for the computer and electronics industry.
<u>Vice President of Operations</u>
Total manufacturing operations of four plants and 600 employees. Other accomplishments:
- Suggested major revision of factory floor operations, decreasing supervisory personnel needs by 20%, increasing quality control.
- Turned around the two major problem plants in company.
- Was able to increase output of plant by 50% with no increased investment.

GENERAL MOTORS, TRANSMISSION OPERATIONS, BUICK DIVISION
Detroit, MI   1973 to 1977
<u>Assistant to Area Manager of Manufacturing</u>   1975 to 1977
Assisted in converting plant's floor operation to "team assembly" operation. Member of 10 person task force to determine if team assembly could be applied to GM operations outside of transmission operation.

<u>Assistant Plant Manager</u>   1973 to 1975
FORD MOTOR CORPORATION, TRANSMISSION OPERATIONS
1971 to 1973
<u>Junior Assistant to Vice President, Plant Facility</u>

EDUCATION:
University of Southern Illinois, 1970.
B.S., Metallurgical Engineering.

PERSONAL: *Date of birth, family situation*
Excellent health.
Wife and I both play string instruments, and we participate in local chamber orchestras.

EXHIBIT 22–B—Continued   131

Richard Collins
626 Horton Avenue
Dayton, OH 45411
(513) 880-2445

Dear Mr. Karson:

I am seeking a position as President or General Manager of a manufacturing company, within either a stable, profitable firm or one that needs a turnaround. My area of expertise is with firms producing metal products for varied applications such as building braces, factory and computer floors, conveyer and factory inventory systems, to name just a few. I am known to implement strong financial control systems. I also bring another important ingredient to bear in this business—a degree in metallurgy.

I have had true general management responsibility for the past 10 years. This position covered complete profit and loss responsibility, as well as total sales, manufacturing, marketing, and financial accountability. The firms ranged in size from $25 million to $75 million. I started out in large firms, Ford Motor and General Motors, where I learned techniques that I have since applied to the smaller operation that I ran. I am a humanistic executive who thrives on teams and developing people. I know what is going on in my operation by "walking the factory floor."

I would like to cite the fact that I have instituted corporate programs that are essential to any firm's growth: namely, cutting personnel operating costs when there is a growing shortage of skilled factory workers. At Brace-It, we introduced extensive training courses for all our people, contributing to profitability in a way that most other efforts (cost-cutting campaigns, new controls) could hardly compare. And this worked for the long term.

My current compensation is in the low six-figure range, and I would be willing to relocate for the right position. I would be pleased to hear from you.

Yours truly,

Richard Collins

EXHIBIT 22–C   Cover Letter/Résumé (General Manager of Manufacturing Company): AFTER

Richard Collins
626 Horton Avenue
Dayton, OH 45411
(513) 880-2445

SUMMARY:

General Manager in manufacturing firms producing diverse light metal products lines. Have been Division General Manager of successful turnaround situations ($25 million to $75 million), transforming nonprofitable organizations into profitable ones. Known to implement strong financial control systems while creating a humanistic environment. Acquired excellent business training at **Ford Motor Co.** and **General Motors**. Bring experience in manufacturing, sales and products serving consumer and industrial markets in both custom made and high volume commodity products.

EDUCATION:

University of Southern Illinois, 1970; B.S., Metallurgical Engineering

PROFESSIONAL EXPERIENCE:

BRACE-IT, Dayton, OH (Sales $55 million)   1987 to Present
Manufacturer and distributor of specialized steel and aluminum bracing products to strengthen walls, floors, and ceilings in overloaded buildings.
Executive Vice President and General Manager
Responsible for aluminum products' profit and loss performance. Accountabilities include marketing, finance, manufacturing, design, research and development, and quality assurance. Some accomplishments:

Finance: Introduced 5 year rolling forecast into firm.
Changed local banks and obtained improved financing arrangements.

Training: Introduced extensive training courses for first time in history of firm. Enabled firm to reduce new hiring program and cut direct and overhead staffing requirements by 16%. Contributed 19% to bottom line.

Sales: Repositioned product lines.
Developed and launched new products for commercial and residential market segments.
In first year, shut down 20% of product lines, increasing profits by 24%.

OKTAL ALUMINUM, Dayton, OH (Sales $75 million)   1986 to 1987
Manufacturer of specialized aluminum products selling to manufacturers of factory floor equipment (conveyers, inventory, etc.)
Executive Vice President and Chief Operating Officer
Multiplant operation, responsible for total profit and loss performance. Some accomplishments:
Finance: Developed and implemented three-year rolling forecast for capital and operational requirements.
Reduced break-even point 25%.

EXHIBIT 22–D   Cover Letter/Résumé (General Manager of Manufacturing Company): AFTER

Sales: Instituted new catalog system, decreasing reliance on local distributors.
Increased total order backlog 75%.

HR: Called for new hiring procedures to enable better evaluation of candidates.

QA   Achieved quality assurance levels of 99% and serviceability rate of 95%.

SPENCER PLATFORMS, Pittsburgh, PA (Sales $25 million) 1980 to 1986
Manufacturer and distributor of special flooring equipment for factory floors.
Vice President and General Manager
Responsible for total division profit and loss performance. Some accomplishments:
-   In first year, made firm profitable after previous two years of loss.
-   Restructured sales force by setting up regional operation to allow direct sales people to be closer to customer.
-   Achieved 25% ROI.
-   Selected and implemented new MIS operation.

MEXLER INDUSTRIES, Indianapolis, IN   1977 to 1980
Manufacturer and distributor of high-quality aluminum fasteners and braces for the computer and electronics industry.
Vice President of Operations
Total manufacturing operations of four plants and 600 employees. Some accomplishments:
-   Suggested major revision of factory floor operations, decreasing supervisory personnel needs by 20%, increasing quality control.
-   Turned around the two major problem plants in company.
-   Was able to increase output of plant by 50% with no increased investment.

GENERAL MOTORS, TRANSMISSION OPERATIONS, BUICK DIVISION
Detroit, MI   1973 to 1977
Assistant to Area Manager of Manufacturing   1975 to 1977
Assisted in converting plant's floor operation to "team assembly" operation.
Member of 10-person task force to determine if team assembly could be applied to GM operations outside of transmission operation.
Assistant Plant Manager   1973 to 1975

FORD MOTOR, TRANSMISSION OPERATIONS   1971 to 1973
Junior Assistant to Vice President, Plant Facility

PERSONAL:
Excellent health. Born June, 1949. Married; have two high school age children.
Wife and I both play string instruments, and we participate in local chamber orchestras.

1440 S. Fourth St.
Ft. Lauderdale, FL 33319
(305) 727-0967

Dear Sir:

I enclosed my résumé should one of your clients be interested in my qualifications. I am seeking an opportunity to manage a company that may wish to achieve one or more of the following goals, such as technical and financial improvement, substantial growth through tight control of quality and overhead costs (allowing new investments to be made), and cultural or organizational modification to meet future market or industry demands.

Since 1979, I have successfully managed several small and medium-sized companies in the IC, semiconductor, and microchip areas. My experience includes new product development, implementation of modern manufacturing methods, company acquisition and disposition plus involvement in tariff and export/import issues in the semiconductor industry. I am known to be a builder of strong, dynamic teams, demanding excellence from myself and my organization. I believe companies should be driven by new and high-quality products, be financially controlled, and be sensitive to market changes.

I am looking forward to hearing from you.

Very truly yours,

Robert Polinski

Should open with statement of "what I am."

As will be seen by the résumé, this person knows thoroughly the IC, semiconductor. and microchip industries. He should state this.

This letter also does not show that he has been a general manager and president and has had 10 years' experience with Intel, a leader in his field, where he learned the business.

EXHIBIT 23–A   Cover Letter/Résumé (President of $50 Million Electronics Firm): BEFORE

Robert Polinski
1440 S. Fourth St.
Ft. Lauderdale, FL 33319
(305) 727-0967

BACKGROUND

A seasoned P&L executive in the custom chip development industry. Have run firms with annual sales in the $50 million range. Am seeking a GM/COO opportunity that requires a bottom-line and marketing oriented team builder with strong insights into technology. *Words, words, words.*

PROFESSIONAL EXPERIENCE

Needs stronger "What I am" to match cover letter.

1986 to Present

Microchips International, Boca Raton, FL (annual sales of $50 million)
General Manager. Full P&L responsibility in the design, manufacture, and marketing of specialized microchips for the communications industry. *← Name firms*
Accomplishments:
Established plans for organizational and cultural modifications to meet the expected technical expansion of VLSI technology segment.
Installed new CAD/CAM operation, resulting in quick response capability to customers.

1982 to 1986

General Chip Design Corporation, Keene, NH (annual sales of $42 million)
1984-1986, President. Complete P&L responsibility in the design of microchips.
1982-1984, Executive Vice President
Accomplishments:
Brought in new R&D team to lead in product development.
Increased sales and profits 15% and 54% respectively.
Developed three-year strategic plan, including shift in firm's direction from a supplier to computer manufacturers to sales to special PCBs. Also changed corporate strategy from being a quality IC firm to one which did microchip design.

Make into list

1971 to 1982

Messy Presentation

Intel Corporation, Santa Clara, CA
1980-1982, Director of Marketing/Sales for division providing memory chips.
1975-79, Marketing/Sales Manager for microprocessors.
1973-1976, Western Regional/International Sales Manager for $100 million region.
1971-1974, Sales person for memory chips.

PERSONAL

Married, three children.
Excellent health.

EDUCATION

University of Illinois, B.S., Industrial Engineering, 1971.
University of California, San Francisco, M.B.A., 1982.

Place at top

EXHIBIT 23–B   Cover Letter/Résumé (President of $50 Million Electronics Firm): BEFORE

1440 S. Fourth St.
Ft. Lauderdale, FL 33319
(305) 727-0967

Dear Mr. Karson:

I am currently president of a $50 million firm specializing in the design and manufacturing of state-of-the-art specialized microchips for the communications industry. This firm is one of the leaders in the country. The firm is being purchased, however, by a giant European firm, and I wish to explore my options prior to making a long-term commitment to stay as president of Microchips International.

Prior to my position at Microchips International, I have had P&L and management responsibility at General Chi Design, and it was at INTEL, where I was for 10 years, that I received my comprehensive training in this field.

I am an expert in the general field of memory chips, semiconductors on microchips using VLSI technology. In addition, my experience includes company acquisition and disposition of mid-sized high-tech firms.

I feel that I am an excellent candidate for president of a firm in the chip industry whose size is between $50 and $250 million. The type of company I would like to manage is one which is seeking:

1.   Technical and financial improvement.
2.   Substantial growth through tight control of quality and overhead costs, thereby allowing new investments to be made.
3.   Cultural or organizational modification to meet future market or industry demands.

An insight into how I manage: I strive to build strong teams, and I believe companies should be driven by new and high-quality products, be financially controlled, and be sensitive to market changes.

I have a B.S. from the University of Illinois in Industrial Engineering and an M.B.A. from the University of California, San Francisco.

My present salary is $115,000, supplemented by a 50 percent performance bonus and various perks. I am 39 years old and have three children. Having lived and managed firms in three different regions in the United States—and having enjoyed all three—relocation is not a problem.

I look forward to receiving your assistance in my exploratory job search.

Sincerely,

Robert Polinski

1440 S. Fourth St.   Ft. Lauderdale, FL 33319   (305) 727-0967

OVERVIEW

General Manager/President of firm ($50 million sales) producing customized microchips: microcomputers, communication chips, and industrial controllers. Know how to compete against the giants, such as Motorola and Intel. Received industry training at **Intel.** Hands-on manager who "touches" all aspects of operation: foundry, design, CAD/CAM, customer relations, technology forecasting, and full range of financial controls. Excellent presentations to financial community—venture capital and investment banks. Am known to be a *catalyst for change.*

EDUCATION

University of Illinois, B.S., Industrial Engineering, 1971.
University of California, San Francisco, M.B.A., 1982.

PROFESSIONAL EXPERIENCE

1986 to Present

Microchips International, Boca Raton, FL
Annual sales of $50 million. Microchips International competes against the majors such as Intel and Motorola, but brings quick reaction time service, coupled with error-free design. Customers include IBM, Unisys, NCR, and Racal Milgo.

General Manager. Full P&L responsibility in the design, manufacture and marketing of specialized microchips for the computer/communications industry.
Accomplishments:
* Established plans for organizational and cultural modifications to meet the expected technical expansion of VLSI technology segment.
* Installed new CAD/CAM operation resulting in quick-response capability to customers.

1982 to 1986

General Chip Design Corporation, Keene, NH
Annual sales of $42 million.

1984-1986, President. Complete P&L responsibility in the design of microchips.
Executive Vice President, 1982-1984
Accomplishments:
* Developed three-year strategic plan including shift in firm's direction from a supplier to computer manufacturers to sales to special PCBs. Also changed corporate strategy from being a quality IC firm to one which did microchip design.
* Brought in new R&D team to lead in product development.
* Increased sales and profits 15% and 54% respectively.

1971 to 1982

Intel Corporation, Santa Clara, CA

Director of Marketing/Sales	1980-1982
Memory chips.	
Marketing/Sales Manager	1975-1979
Microprocessors.	
Western Regional/International Sales Manager	1973-1976
$100 million region.	
Salesperson	1971-1973
Memory chips.	

PERSONAL

Married; three children; excellent health.

EXHIBIT 23–D   *Cover Letter/Résumé (President of $50 Million Electronic Firm): AFTER*

Norman Gelman
1880 Rugby Road
Boston, MA 02113

Dear Mr. Karson:

It is time for me to seek a position in a bigger firm. The positions for which I am qualified include chief information officer and senior vice president for MIS.

I am currently Vice President of MIS for Bridge Finance Corporation, a modest-sized financial services firm serving consumer industries in the Boston area. I am responsible for data processing, voice and data communications, office automation, distributed and personal computing—an operation with a $12 million budget employing 130 professionals.

Since joining Bridge, I have been responsible for strategic and short-term planning and running the data center. Within this domain, I have extensive experience integrating and managing complex systems which involve networks of mainframes (IBM 4300s), minis (DEC VAXs), micros (Convergent Technologies and IBM PC compatibles) and telephone systems (Siemens).

Prior to being with Bridge, I turned two poorly performing MIS departments into leadership positions within their firms. I replaced an inward MIS directed management culture with one that was outward directed; that is, servicing the users of the system (our customers). Some of the methods I introduced were:

-   Training courses on MIS effectiveness as seen in case studies based on operations at Merrill Lynch, American Express, and Citibank.
-   Semiannual individual performance reviews—for all levels of people (me included)—based on peer and subordinate evaluations.
-   Keeping an open shop for vendors by welcoming them to make presentations about their products, enabling us to learn new system solutions.

In all my management activities, I have sought to meet the needs of employees and management by initiating quality circles, setting up large spans of control, flattening out management hierarchies, and introducing self-managing teams. In my present responsibility, I made the MIS department completely responsive to the needs of our internal customers by cutting down system-solution waiting time by 50 percent.

I hold a B.S. in Business Administration and Computer Science from the State University of New York at Stony Brook and have numerous professional certifications. I received my M.S. in Management Information Systems from Babson College in Wellesley, MA.

EXHIBIT 24 Cover Letter Accompanying a Résumé (Vice President—MIS) **139**

I am seeking a position in a large firm. I wish to run a large information system organization where IS is an integral part of corporate operations, an organization that shows the various departments how IS can better serve their needs, whether in sales, marketing, finance, manufacturing, human resources, or administration.

I want to build, rebuild, or significantly develop an MIS department into a high-performing business unit. I seek a challenge where performance is matched by rewards.

To assist you in determining where I fit in within your clients' needs, my compensation has been $130,000 plus a group of corporate perks. My home phone is (617) 666-2344. I Thank you in advance for your assistance.

Yours truly,

Norman Gelman

Although this is a relatively long cover letter, I like its style. It clearly tells what this person is. The letter is light and informative.

WARNING: If you choose to write a similar expository letter, make sure it is not dense. If it is dense in terms of subject and format, no one will read it.

EXHIBIT 24—Continued

PAUL F. MAZARINI
36 Warren Lane
Raleigh, NC 27629
(919) 332-6432

Dear Mr. Karson:

I would appreciate your reviewing my enclosed résumé to determine whether one of your clients is seeking a person with my background and expertise.

I have been in the investment banking community for more than 20 years. This covers most aspects of the financial services industry. My background as a commercial loan officer at an investment bank demonstrates an outstanding blend of financial, market development, conceptual, and administrative abilities. Previous positions included participation on the loan committee of a $12 billion asset bank.

Concurrent to the loan operations, I developed a leasing plan for a quickly growing computer manufacturer and managed a leasing subsidiary which directly resulted in an 8 percent profit increase to the bank within one year. This latter program included a computer lease seminar directed to computer users, computer manufacturers, as well as personnel within the bank.

I have received numerous plaudits from bank officers and key industrial clients concerning my contribution. These attest to a proven record of successful product innovation, supported by sound credit and marketing capabilities.

I will be calling you within the next week to discuss possible opportunities within your client firms.

Sincerely,

Paul F. Mazarini

This is a fair letter that could be improved by stating title and salary to show where the person is in the hierarchical system. Lacks mention of client names and markets (except computer leasing).

Letter should also be used to "elevate" person within business community.

EXHIBIT 25–A   *Cover Letter/Résumé (Commercial Loan Officer): BEFORE*   141

PAUL F. MAZARINI
36 Warren Lane
Raleigh, NC 27629
Home (919) 332-6432
Office (919) 962-1100

Good presentation.
Opportunity to make more
interesting by including
brand names.

SUMMARY

Marketing and product-oriented banking professional with extensive experience in corporate finance and industrial leasing products. Provided leadership, sound judgment, and creativity in business generation and innovative applications of credit standards to a wide variety of financial instruments. Have worked closely with chemical, computer industry, and high-tech firms in Eastern U.S.

← Words, words, words.

EXPERIENCE

NCNB CORPORATION, Charlotte, NC   **1986-Present**

Vice President, Market Development
Responsible for marketing financial products to Eastern North Carolina. The products included mortgages for shopping centers, industrial expansion, harbor and airport development, and fishery development. Expanded customer base within region by 19%. All of these are non-speculative opportunities providing minimum risk financing.

Name some
locations —
or an event.

NCNB INVESTMENT BANK

Manager for high-technology industry. Participated in marketing of mortgage-backed securities and collateralized mortgage obligations. Provided extensive market updates and product knowledge of the industry.

- Established over $1 billion in loan portfolios.
- Managed three $60 million transactions in concert with three regional banks.
- Initiated and completed 14 commercial loan transactions with Golden-Triangle high-tech firms. *← Name some.*

BOSTON BANCORP CAPITOL MARKETS, Boston, MA   **1984-1986**

Vice President
Directed sourcing and marketing of loan portfolios, securities, and various asset-backed securities. Account base included pension funds, thrifts, and banks.

- Originated deal, obtained bids, and closed on a $250 million third party originated computer lease portfolio.
- Developed new department to expand bank's participation in leveraged buyouts.
- Developed a data base to facilitate analysis of credit requests, using prior bank techniques and those favored by other regional banks.
- Conducted training seminars for corporate and bank personnel on leasing.

BURLINGTON BANK OF MASSACHUSETTS, Burlington, MA   **1980-1984**

Vice President, Corporate Banking Group *Name Some*
Supervised portfolio of industrial clients within the corporate group. Credit facilities included revolving lines, term loans, lease debt funding, and asset-based leasing. Was member of the Senior Loan Committee. Implemented the first leasing subsidiary of the bank, resulting in an increased profit in bank operations of 23% within first year.

GIRARD BANK, Philadelphia, PA   **1970-1980**

Officer for Special Chemical and Industrial Loans 1976-1980 *Names*

Corporate liaison officer to Mid-Atlantic chemical firms for inventory lines of credit. Presented and implemented all regional rates and credit recommendations. Presented and recommended credit requests to general loan committee.

Internal Auditor, Credit Operation   1973-1976
Reviewed and monitored loan portfolio quality of the bank's Mid-Atlantic region. Set up procedures and data base to clarify loans by quality and size. Performed on-site analysis of major and risky loans.

Assistant Supervisor, Harrisburg Branch   1970-1973
Reviewed loans for regional railroad firms, developing high-tech firms and specialized steel operations. Supervised three employees, ultimately expanding operation to seven people.

EDUCATION

Urania College, Reading, PA, 1970.
B.S., Accounting.

EXHIBIT 25–B—Continued   143

PAUL F. MAZARINI
36 Warren Lane
Raleigh, NC 27629
(919) 332-6432

Dear Mr. Karson:

I would appreciate your reviewing my enclosed résumé to determine whether one of your clients would be interested in a person with my background and expertise. I am seeking a position in a regional bank wherein I would have overall responsibility for market development within the industrial sector.

I am currently vice president for market development at the NCNB Corporation, responsible for marketing financial products to Eastern North Carolina's shopping centers, industrial expansion, harbor and airport development, and fishery development. I would say that my major strength is the creation of diverse programs for a wide range of industries, ranging from rust-belt to high-technology firms.

Prior to the present market development position, I was NCNB's manager for the high-technology industry, dealing with such firms as IBM, Northern Telecom and a host of dynamic technology start up companies in pharmaceuticals and genetics. I have an excellent understanding of the U.S. industry-at-large, starting with the Girard Bank of Philadelphia, where I specialized in the chemical, high-tech, and steel industries.

Also, over the years I have developed a special affinity for and understanding of the leasing business. As an example, I developed at Burlington Bank a leasing plan for a highly successful specialized computer manufacturer, Masscomp, which enabled the firm to develop quickly. I also managed the bank's leasing subsidiary, which directly resulted in an 8 percent profit increase to the Burlington within one year.

I continually receive numerous plaudits from many CEOs in industry concerning my contribution to their firm and my understanding of their particular needs. Based on this understanding, I have always been able to attract major accounts.

My current remuneration is $135,000 plus a bonus of 35 percent which is based on both personal and bank performance.

I will be calling you within the next week to discuss possible opportunities within your client firms.

Sincerely.

Roger P. Mazarini

PAUL F. MAZARINI
36 Warren Lane
Raleigh, NC 27629
Home (919) 332-6432
Office (919) 962-1100

SUMMARY

Market Development Bank Executive who has specialized in investment and leasing programs for East Coast industry. Extensive top-level contacts within computer, communication, genetic, pharmaceutical, and steel sectors. Within all positions, such as with **NCNB, Boston Bancorp** and **Girard Bank,** have created innovative loan and leasing programs which have had a direct impact on both my firm and its industrial clients.

EXPERIENCE

1986-Present   **NCNB CORPORATION, Charlotte, NC**

Vice President, Market Development   1988-Present
Responsible for marketing financial products to Eastern North Carolina. The products included mortgages for shopping centers, industrial expansion, harbor (Wilmington) and airport development (Raleigh-Durham and Elizabeth City), and fishery development. Worked with regional insurance firms to assist in reestablishing havoc-ridden areas following Hurricane *Hugo.* Expanded customer base within region by 19%. All of these are non-speculative opportunities providing minimum risk financing.

NCNB INVESTMENT BANK   1986-1988

Manager for high-technology industry
Participated in marketing of mortgage-backed securities and collateralized mortgage obligations. Maintained close contact with industrial leaders and trade groups to have first-hand sense of health of firms (through club memberships, the Roundtable, industry-focused seminars, and extensive personal network of industry CFOs and CEOs). Provided guidance throughout firm on industrial loans.
- Established over $1 billion in loan portfolios.
- Managed three $60 million transactions in concert with three regional banks.
- Initiated and completed 14 commercial loan transactions with Golden-Triangle high-tech firms, including Northern Telecom, IBM and manufacturers of genetic categorization systems.

1984-1986   **BOSTON BANCORP CAPITAL MARKETS, Boston, MA**

Vice President
Directed sourcing and marketing of loan portfolios, securities, and various asset-backed securities. Account base included pension funds, thrifts and banks.
- Originated deal, obtained bids, and closed on a $250 million third-party originated computer lease portfolio.
- Developed new department to expand bank's participation in leveraged buyouts.
- Developed a data base to facilitate analysis of credit requests, using prior bank techniques and those favored by other regional banks.
- Conducted training seminars for corporate and bank personnel on leasing.

1980-1984 **BURLINGTON BANK OF MASSACHUSETTS, Burlington, MA**

Vice President, Corporate Banking Group
- Supervised portfolio of industrial clients within the corporate group. Credit facilities included revolving lines, term loans, lease debt funding, and asset-based leasing.
- Set up highly successful relationships with Boston computer industry, assisting many firms, including Masscomp, Apollo, and Interlan.
- Implemented the first leasing subsidiary of the bank, resulting in an increased profitability in bank operations of 23% within first year.
- Was member of the Senior Loan Committee.

1970-1980 **GIRARD BANK, Philadelphia, PA**

Officer for Special Chemical and Industrial Loans 1976-1980
Corporate liaison officer to Mid-Atlantic chemical firms (ICI and DuPont) for inventory lines of credit. Presented and implemented all regional rates and credit recommendations. Presented and recommended credit requests to general loan committee.

Internal Auditor, Credit Operation 1973-1976
Reviewed and monitored loan portfolio quality of the bank's Mid-Atlantic region. Set up procedures and data base to clarify loans by quality and size. Performed on-site analysis of major and risky loans.

Assistant Supervisor, Harrisburg Branch 1970-1973
Reviewed loans for regional railroad firms, developing high tech firms and specialized steel operations. Supervised three employees, ultimately expanding operation to seven people.

EDUCATION

Urania College, Reading, PA, 1970.
B.S., Accounting.

ROLLIN TRUMBELL
44 Lake Drive
Cleveland, OH 44165
(216) 885-1690

Dear Mr. Karson:

My business career has been as a leader in the tool industry, leading small-to-medium sized firms to profitability. If you are seeking a success-oriented corporate division president to add strong hands-on operating expertise and industry knowledge to one of your client companies, I would be most interested in discussing this with you.

For the last nine years, I have served as a senior executive of Acme Cleveland, Inc., a highly profitable $250 million leader in the tools industry. My most recent assignment was as president of two of its wholly owned subsidiaries with combined annual sales of $60 million. In one division, financial performance exceeded plan by 40 percent while the division's output doubled in less than two years. A major turnaround was accomplished in the other division, reducing losses from nearly $2 million to break-even in 18 months.

As Vice President of Operations for the $120 million AC Telecommunications division, a manufacturer of tools for the electrical industry, I was responsible for managing a multiplant environment. The executive committee provided me with a corporate citation, indicating that this was the finest run division operation ever, within the 30 year history of the firm.

Due to recent changes in the management structure, which have reduced the number of upward career paths that are available, I have decided to leave and explore other business and acquisition opportunities. Please call me if I can help you achieve your objectives.

Sincerely,

Rollin Trumbell

A good letter that could be improved by citing some of the management specialties of the person. Salary would also help the reader understand the level the person is seeking.

ROLLIN TRUMBELL
44 Lake Drive
Cleveland, OH 44165
(216) 885-1690

No good. "What I am" is needed

OBJECTIVE

My primary objective is to manage a business with sales between $40 and $100 million.

RECENT PROFESSIONAL ACCOMPLISHMENTS

Good

1. As President of two subsidiaries (with $60 million revenues) of Acme Cleveland, specializing in high-quality machine tools for the commercial market, I was responsible for exceeding financial performance expectations by 60% while tripling the company's output over a two-year period.

2. As Vice President of Manufacturing at AC Telecommunications, a $120 million subsidiary of Acme Cleveland, I was assigned to turn around an out-of-control loss situation. In 18 months, losses were cut from nearly $15 million to a virtual break-even.

3. As Vice President of Manufacturing at AC Telecommunications, I successfully produced a record annual number of new product introductions during a period in which corporate profitability achieved record high levels. [I was responsible, through a staff of four direct subordinates, for planning and coordinating the purchasing, production control, shop floor production, manufacturing, engineering, and distribution groups.] This multiplant organization contained over 200 employees, with an annual manufacturing budget of over $80 million.

Delete. Not appropriate since this is assumed to be the responsibility for such a position

EMPLOYMENT HISTORY

1980-Present: ACME CLEVELAND, INCORPORATED   Cleveland, OH

Acme Cleveland is a publicly held, $250 million manufacturer and marketer of machine tools and telecommunications products. I have had five progressively more important positions, including:
- President, AC Tools, Inc. and AC Home Tools, Inc., 1986-Present.
- Vice President, Operations, AC Telecommunications, 1983-86.
- Vice President, Planning, AC Telecommunications, 1982-83.
- Director of Warehousing, 1980-81.

Served as an inside director for the Boards of Directors of both AC Tools, Inc. and AC Home Tools, Inc., wholly owned subsidiaries of Acme Cleveland.

EXHIBIT 26–B *Cover Letter/Résumé (President/General Manager of $60 Million Industrial): BEFORE*

1977-1980:   BROWN & SHARP CORPORATION   North Kingston, RI

Brown & Sharp is a $300 million, multiplant manufacturer of precision measuring instruments and machine tools equipment. As manager of inventory systems, I was responsible for a staff of ninety employees in the inventory control, receiving/warehousing, and purchasing administration groups. Implemented an integrated materials requirements planning (MRP) system in these areas as part of a larger, company-wide project.

Needs better presentation

1965-1977:   L. S. STARRETT CORPORATION   Athol, MA

L.S. Starrett is a $250 million manufacturer of metrology tools, instruments, and other varied products.
- 1973-77 Manager of Purchasing, Instrument Products Dept.
This department was a $60 million manufacturer of calipers and gauges for the industrial market.
- 1972-73 New Products, Planning, Instrument Production.
- 1967-72 Manager of Materials, Director of Materials.
- 1965-67 Manufacturing Management Program
During this two year training program, I served in six different manufacturing positions at different plant locations. Position assignments included Inventory Analyst, Shop Foreman, Manufacturing Control, Production Engineer, Quality Control, and Materials Management.

History. Delete.

EDUCATION

B.B.A., University of Massachusetts, Amherst, MA, 1965.

Manufacturing Management Program, 1967.
This two-year program combined classroom work with separate on-the-job training assignments involving progressively greater responsibilities.

This is history. It also detracts from an "executive image". Delete.

EXHIBIT 26–B—Continued   149

ROLLIN TRUMBELL
44 Lake Drive
Cleveland, OH 44165
(216) 885-1690

Dear Mr. Karson:

My business career has been as a leader in the tool industry, leading small to medium-sized firms to profitability. Due to recent changes in my firm's management that have reduced the number of upward career paths that are available, I have decided to explore business opportunities where I can manage a business with sales between $40 and $100 million.

For the last nine years, I have served as a senior executive of Acme Cleveland, Inc., a highly profitable $250 million leader in the tools industry. My most recent assignment was president of two of Acme 's wholly owned subsidiaries with combined annual sales of $60 million. In one division, financial performance exceeded plan by 40 percent while the division's output doubled in less than two years. A major turnaround was accomplished in the other division, reducing losses from nearly $2 million to break-even in 18 months.

As Vice President of Operations, for Acme's $120 million AC Telecommunications division, a manufacturer of tools for the electrical industry, I was responsible for managing a multiplant environment. The executive committee indicated that this was the finest run division operation, ever, within the thirty-year history of the firm.

My specialty is plant operations including everything from sophisticated MRP systems to scrap control, from knowing what is manufacturable to insisting on excellence in quality control, encompassing all aspects of plant operation, product manufacturing, and back-office operations. I have benefited from being with excellent firms, having worked with the best people in the industry at L.S. Starrett and Brown & Sharp.

 Please call me if you have a situation that may apply to me.

While salary is not the most important feature that I seek, my family and I are accustomed to a life-style that accompanies a remuneration package of $150,000, supplemented by various corporate perks.

I do look forward to hearing from you in the near future.

Sincerely,

Rollin Trumbell

EXHIBIT 26–C   Cover Letter/Résumé (President/General Manager of $60 Million Industrial): AFTER

ROLLIN TRUMBELL
44 Lake Drive
Cleveland, OH 44165
(216) 885-1690

OVERVIEW

General Manager/COO in the tool industry. Have worked for industry leaders: Acme Cleveland, Brown & Sharp, and L. S. Starrett. Specialty is multiplant plant operations: MRP systems, manufacturing engineering, quality control, and running tight cost-control operations. Management style is to keep in close contact with all aspects of the operation and to create a no-surprise business operation.

EMPLOYMENT HISTORY

1980-Present **ACME CLEVELAND, INCORPORATED,** Cleveland, OH
Acme Cleveland is a publicly held, $250 million manufacturer and marketer of machine tools and telecommunications products. Originally introduced to Acme by its lead bank, Bank One Cleveland, to assist in introducing new inventory control and warehousing systems. Since then, have had five progressively more important positions:
- President, AC Tools, Inc. and AC Home Tools, Inc. 1986-Present
- Vice President, Operations, AC Telecom. 1983-86
- Vice President, Planning, AC Telecom. 1982-83
- Director of Warehousing. 1980-81
- Inside director for the boards of directors of both AC Tools, Inc. and AC Home Tools, Inc., wholly owned subsidiaries of Acme Cleveland.

RECENT ACCOMPLISHMENTS AT ACME CLEVELAND

President of two subsidiaries (with $60 million revenues), specializing in high-quality machine tools for the commercial market. Responsible for exceeding financial performance expectations by 60% while tripling the company's output over a two-year period.

Vice President of Manufacturing at AC Telecommunications, a $120 million subsidiary producing tools for the electrical industry. Turned around an out-of-control loss situation. In 18 months, losses were cut from nearly $15 million to a virtual break-even.

Vice-President, Manufacturing of AC Telecommunications. Produced a record annual number of new product introductions during a period in which corporate profitability achieved record high levels. This multiplant organization contained over 200 employees, with an annual manufacturing budget of over $80 million.

ROLLIN TRUMBELL

1977-1980 **BROWN & SHARP CORPORATION,** North Kingston, RI
Brown & Sharp is a $300 million, multiplant manufacturer of precision measuring instruments and machine tools equipment.

Manager of Inventory Systems Responsible for a staff of 90 employees in the inventory control, receiving/warehousing, and purchasing administration groups. Implemented an integrated materials requirements planning (MRP I) system in these areas as part of a larger, companywide project.

1965-1977 **L. S. STARRETT CORPORATION**, Athol, MA

L.S. Starrett is a $250 million manufacturer of metrology tools, instruments, and other varied products.
- Manager of Purchasing, Instrument Products Dept.   1973-77
  This department was a $60 million manufacturer of calipers and gauges for the industrial market.
- New Products, Planning, Instrument Production.   1972-73
- Manager of Materials, Director of Materials.   1967-72
- Manufacturing Management Program.   1965-67

EDUCATION

B.B.A., University of Massachusetts, Amherst, MA, 1965.
Manufacturing Management Program, 1967.

13121 Pacific Heights
San Francisco, CA 94148

Dear Mr. Karson:

I am a successful senior executive in the banking industry with more than 20 years of diverse management experience in increasingly more responsible positions. My skills and experience include:

- Bank general management—with P&L
- Executive advisor responsibilities dealing with strategic issues and market development.
- Management, planning, and operations background in credit card and financial service industry.
- Managing large-scale electronics data processing operations activities.

This background makes me appropriate for:

- CEO or COO of a financial organization.
- General manager of a national or regional financial services or related organization.
- General management of a major information system.

My strengths are managing people and managing to the bottom line. I am a team builder and am known for high integrity. My strengths are in managing a profit-oriented operation and taking advantage of the benefits that technology can provide in running an information based operation. My experience has primarily been in the banking services industry, but I consider my executive skills are applicable to other financially oriented service industries.

While compensation is not a critical issue if the opportunity has long range potential, please note that my current compensation is $185,000, supplemented by various bonus opportunities.

I would like to schedule a discussion with you to determine how my background and experience might fit your clients' needs. Please call me at home during the evening at (415)681-2232.

Sincerely,

Sanford J. McPherson

```
This could be considered a good cover letter, but it does not adequately
point out the key strength of the person, i.e., expertise, success and
leadership in the credit card system industry.

The paragraph beginning, "My strengths..." is words, words, words.

The cover letter should also contain the names of the excellent financial
institutions for which he worked.
```

EXHIBIT 27–A   Cover Letter/Résumé (Bank Executive, Credit Card Sector): BEFORE

Fair presentation which can be improved by stronger "What I am."

Sanford J. McPherson
13121 Pacific Heights
San Francisco, CA 94148
(415) 681-2232

BACKGROUND

A senior banking executive with a broad and depthful background in managing varied financial service operations: credit card operations for regional banks and for a major bank, complete commercial bank operations, market development, and major information systems. Have also provided strategic guidance in many key bank-related operations.

BUSINESS EXPERIENCE

Words, words, words. Lacks brand names.

BANK OF AMERICA CREDIT CARD SERVICES, San Francisco, CA   1986-Present
A subsidiary of Bank of America Corporation.

Executive-Vice President
Took over a faltering high-cost credit card operation and in first year brought costs to where they were in line with revenue; in second year attained profitable operation. Presently the operation has the highest rate of growth and profit margins of any bank credit card operation in the West.

Good

Redefined how the credit card service is sold both to local banks as a support facility and to consumers. Established statewide boutiques to acquaint affluent customers with the relative merits of the B of A card in comparison to other bank cards and promoted use of card within corporate accounts. Increased volume by 46% while continuing to use present system facilities.

WORLD BANK, Washington, D.C.   1985-1986

Senior Advisor (temporary assignment)
Requested by Bank's chief of strategy to provide strategic guidance to developing nations on how they could enhance their financial service infrastructure through the use of credit card services.

San Francisco Charter Bank, San Francisco, CA   1982-1985
A subsidiary of Bay Area Financial Corporation.

Senior Vice-President, Banking Operations
Directed all major activities of the bank, including commercial and retail loan operations, marketing, human resource functions. Decreased exposure the bank had in critical loan areas (Latin America and petroleum industries) to $15 million from $380 million. Bank operations involved 615 employees.

Initiated a special "Single Person" account that generated over 2,000 new accounts and $12 million in deposits within 90 days.

Not "executive image". Delete

EXHIBIT 27-B   Cover Letter/Résumé (Bank Executive, Credit Card Sector): BEFORE

CCPI, INC., Denver, CO   1975-1982
A credit card processing company serving more than 60
financial institutions in the Western Region and 1.2 million card holders.

President and Chief Executive Officer

Directed the plan for acquiring the next generation system, while simultaneously
expanding system users by 30%.

Present as a list.

Some results of the action plan were: Increased revenue by 27% per year compounded, a
13% reduction of staff on a comparable volume basis, improved service levels by 20%,
reduced transaction processing unit costs by 18%.

Presided over three industry symposia and published "white paper" describing the
challenges to the credit card industry.

IPSWITCH CORPORATION, Boulder, CO   1964-1975
A $2 billion asset regional bank holding company.

Executive Vice-President and Director of Corporate Planning (1971-1975)
Directed the long-range strategic planning process of the Ipswitch Corporation.
Coordinated the bank's new product/services development as well as the review of all
major business development activities.

Vice-President of Corporate MIS Operation (1968-1971)

Responsible for information system planning and operations covering data entry,
computer operations, telecommunications, and software development. [Managed 20
professionals (system programmers), 10 data entry persons, and 10 facility operators.] *Delete*

Assistant Vice-President MIS Operation (1967-1968).
Managed switching from IBM 705 to IBM 360/40 installation. ← *Ancient history*
Computer Services Officer (1966-1967)
Performed feasibility studies to determine new systems the bank was to install. ← *Leave out*
Assistant Loan Officer (1964-1966)
Entry-level position to learn of needs and structure of local economy. ← *to "up-scale image."*

EDUCATION

Advanced Management Program, Stanford University.
M.B.A., University of California at San Francisco, 1968.
B.B.A., Marketing, University of California at Berkeley, 1963.

EXHIBIT 27–B—Continued   155

13121 Pacific Heights
San Francisco, CA 94148

Dear Mr. Karson:

I am a bank executive with significant leadership experience in credit card operations and bank information systems, in addition to general management of commercial bank operations. I have provided this leadership at such organizations as Bank of America, CCPI of Denver, Colorado, and San Francisco Charter Bank. All the activities I have managed have been profitable and the teams we built are among the best in the nation.

And recently during a temporary assignment at the request of the World Bank, I expanded my geographic horizons—and my personal contacts— dealing with developing nations' financial service infrastructure.

Thus, I see my future in terms of:
- Management, planning, and operations background in credit card and financial service industry or in bank information systems.
- Bank general management—with P&L.
- Executive advisor responsibilities dealing with strategic issues and market development.

This background makes me appropriate for:
- CEO or COO of a financial organization.
- General manager of a national or regional financial services or related organization.
- General management of a major information system.

While compensation is not a critical issue if the opportunity has long-range potential, please note that my current compensation is $185,000 supplemented by various bonus opportunities.

I would like to schedule a discussion with you to determine how my background and experience might fit your clients' needs. Please call me at home during the evening at (415) 681-2232.

Sincerely,

Sanford J. McPherson

EXHIBIT 27–C   *Cover Letter/Résumé (Bank Executive, Credit Card Sector):*
AFTER

Sanford J. McPherson
13121 Pacific Heights
San Francisco, CA 94148
(415) 681-2232

BACKGROUND

Bank Executive with significant leadership experience in credit card operations and bank information systems. All the activities I have managed have been profitable, and the teams we built are among the best in the nation. Significant credit card operations at Bank of America and CCPI. In addition, have managed complete commercial bank operations (San Francisco Charter Bank). Developed worldwide contacts during special assignment at World Bank.

EDUCATION

Advanced Management Program, Stanford University.
M.B.A., University of California at San Francisco, 1968.
B.B.A., Marketing, University of California at Berkeley, 1963.

BUSINESS EXPERIENCE

1986-Present **BANK OF AMERICA CREDIT CARD SERVICES**, San Francisco, CA
A subsidiary of Bank of America Corporation.

Executive Vice-President
Took over a faltering high-cost credit card operation. In first year brought costs to where they were in line with revenue, and in second year attained profitable operation. Presently the operation has the highest rate of growth and profit margins of any bank credit card operation in the West.

Redefined how the credit card service is sold both to local banks as a support facility and to consumers. Established statewide boutiques to acquaint affluent customers with the relative merits of the B of A card in comparison to other bank cards and promote use of card within corporate accounts. Increased volume by 46% while continuing to use present system facilities.

1985-1986 **WORLD BANK**, Washington, D.C.

Senior Advisor (temporary assignment)
Requested by Bank's chief of strategy to provide strategic guidance to developing nations on how they could enhance their financial service infrastructure through the use of credit card services.

EXHIBIT 27–D   *Cover Letter/Résumé (Bank Executive, Credit Card Sector):*
AFTER

1982-1985   **SAN FRANCISCO CHARTER BANK,** San Francisco, CA
A subsidiary of Bay Area Financial Corporation.
<u>Senior Vice-President, Banking Operations</u>
Directed all major activities of the bank, including commercial and retail loan operations, marketing, human resource functions. Decreased exposure the bank had in critical loan areas (Latin America and petroleum industries) to $15 million from $380 million. Bank operations involved 615 employees.

1975-1982   **CCPI, INC.,** Denver, CO
A credit card processing company serving more than 60 financial institutions in the Western region and 1.2 million card holders.

<u>President and Chief Executive Officer</u>
Presided over three industry symposia and published "white paper" describing the challenges to the credit card industry.

Directed the plan for acquiring the next generation system, while simultaneously expanding system users by 30%.
Some results of the plan were:
* Increased revenue by 27% per year compounded.
* Achieved 13% reduction of staff on a comparable volume basis.
* Improved service levels by 20%.
* Reduced transaction processing unit costs by 18%.

1964-1975   **IPSWITCH CORPORATION,** Boulder, CO
A regional bank holding company.

<u>Executive Vice President and Director of Planning</u>   1971-1975
Directed the long-range strategic planning process of the Ipswitch Corporation. Coordinated the bank's new product/services development as well as the review of all major business development activities.

<u>Vice President of Corporate MIS Operation</u>   1968-1971
Responsible for information system planning and operations covering data entry, computer operations, telecommunications, and software development.

<u>Assistant Vice President,</u> MIS Operation   1967-1968
<u>Computer Services Officer</u>   1966-1967
<u>Assistant Loan Officer</u>   1964-1966

PROFESSIONAL ACTIVITIES

Member of ABA's credit card executive committee.
Member of World Bank advisory committee on credit card operations.
Frequently called upon to be guest speaker at credit card interest group meetings.

Richard Kenneth Leedermann
2349 West Gate Road
Chevy Chase, MD 20814
(301)442-0607

Dear Mr. Karson:

My background and experience may be attractive to one of your client searches. I believe that the accompanying résumé indicates clearly my areas of expertise.

If you find background to be similar to the specifications that you are now working on and with a compensation package in the $400,000 to $500,000 range, please call. I hope to hear from you soon.

Sincerely,

Richard Kenneth Leedermann

Many of the résumés I receive from highly paid people are accompanied by a cover letter as cryptic as this one. (Their résumés are typically very good, clear, and to the point.) The senders probably feel that their salary alone will entice the reader to continue to examine the résumé in detail to see if there is a plan for the person in the organization, a role that may be different from what they currently have. They are right.

The cover letter, however, will make a more appropriate "executive introduction" by defining the person's areas of expertise, the firms, the schools and the business areas he has been associated with. This will also also help the reader to assess quickly the relevance and applicability of the person.

Richard Kenneth Leedermann
2349 West Gate Road
Chevy Chase, MD 20814
(301)442-0607

Dear Mr. Karson:

My background and experience may be attractive to one of your client company searches. Additional information is certainly available through a telephone call or a personal meeting.

For the past three years, I have been an executive vice president of the Marriott Corporation, where my major influence has been in defining Marriott's expansion and acquisition program. I was instrumental in setting up Marriott's new Courtyard Hotel program. Prior to coming to Marriott, I was an executive at American Airlines responsible for all of its non-airline businesses. My background, expertise, and contacts in the hotel and travel industry are extensive.

I am a graduate of Williams College, have an M.B.A. from Cornell University and have recently supplemented my management experience at the Executive Management Program at Columbia University.

If you are presently providing services to an organization with specifications similar to my background with a compensation package exceeding $500,000, please contact me.

I am looking forward to further discussions with you.

Sincerely,

Richard Kenneth Leedermann

PART VI

LOOKING FOR A JOB WITH YOUR BRAND NAME RESUME
General Advice and Thoughts about the Job Search

You are not just looking for a job.
You are *in the business* of looking for a job.
Act accordingly.
Follow these suggestions on good business practices.

Your first step is to prepare your résumé and basic cover letter. After that, you will have it printed up, mail it and expect responses by telephone or mail. The following sections contain some suggestions you should consider during these various stages.

SECTION 1:   Presentation of Your Résumé

Paper and Printing

- Never use cheap copy paper for your résumé.
- To print your résumé, use the photo offset process or a high-quality copier—do not settle for a cheap copy job.
- Prepare your work on a word processor. You will be changing your résumé so you need the flexibility the word processor provides.
- If you use a word processor, use a letter-quality printer for your cover letter and résumé. Near-letter-quality printers are not used in business for correspondence. A laser printer does wonders. The envelope address can be printed on a label, using near-letter-quality printers.
- Use a high-quality bond paper—the kind lawyers, high-paid business consultant firms, and CEOs use.

    My personal preference for paper is crisp-wove bond paper. I wonder why so many people use laid bond as opposed to wove bond. Most business letters, such as those sent by corporate executives for their own business correspondence, are printed on wove. (Laid bond has small ridges on it; wove bond does not have any ridges.)
- Do not use a dark-colored paper. Hopefully, your cover letter and résumé will be copied and circulated throughout the firm and dark paper may not copy well.

- Use your own personal stationery. Do not use your present firm's stationery. Using that stationery can be considered as misrepresenting you. And it is *you* that you are selling, not your firm.
- The best CLRs—including those submitted by top corporate executives—consist of a one-page, typed cover letter with a résumé of one to two pages (sometimes three is all right). They do not include photographs. A bound folder is superfluous. These CLRs are folded and inserted into 4 1/8-inch by 9 1/2-inch envelopes.
- Do not include letters of recommendation. Doing so reeks of institutional and civil-service thinking.

Presentation

- Read an article on how to make attractive business presentations—an article prepared by a printer or an ad firm.
- Vary type style to make your résumé stand out— and memorable. A well-placed, thin, solid black line can do wonders to highlight sections. Use artistic flair sparingly.

Cover Letters

- Make your cover letter short and to-the-point. It should contain no more than three or four points—presented clearly and succinctly. Strong points about you—what you are and what you seek.
- Use straightforward English, no flowery phrases. Do not try to be erudite or eloquent. Use American English, not Shakespearean English.
- This is a business letter. Do not be cute, funny or overly friendly.
- Do not include a long build-up about why you are looking. The longer a build-up the less believable it becomes. For example, "After 30 years with my current employer, I have decided to make a career change. . ." No one will believe you. Better to say, "My company is in a downswing, and I am now seeking a new position." Or indicate that you are limited in your opportunities for advancement. You didn't say you were fired, considered incompetent after all these years, took early retirement, etc., you have maintained your dignity in the letter—and you did not lie.

Ancillary Items on a Résumé

- Why do so many people list a broad range of hobbies and interests? (If you do include hobbies and interests, list only those you are serious about.)
- If you include a personal interest, make sure you can back it up in strength. Reading the *Wall Street Journal* and your industry's journals does not qualify you to list reading as an interest. (Reading your industry's journals is a *given*.)
- *References on request*. Why bother saying it? It takes up space, and it's also a given.

• Nearly ever résumé says, "excellent health." I would like to see this done away with since, in fact, most people have something that bothers them.

SECTION 2:   Protocol and Doing Things Differently

There is a certain protocol involved in the communication between you and your potential employer. A protocol is a *procedure* that society considers as the way to relate to other people. You have experienced protocols in dating, in meeting a potential client for the first time—and in many other forms of social behavior.[10]

A protocol helps maximize the amount of information you wish to convey while minimizing clutter information and, most importantly, it is expected by the party you are communicating with. It conforms to society's conventions.

In your search for a job, you submit your cover letter and résumé. The information conveyed therein consists of:

• Personal biographical facts (name, phone number, family situation and the like.)
• Personal identification (What you are)
• Position sought
• Recent salary
• Education
• Job history

If the person receiving your correspondence is interested in you, he or she will call you to ask for additional information concerning these features of your background.

I would therefore like to advise people who are considering not following the standard protocol of sending both a cover letter and a résumé.

If you are not a brand name—or have not established yourself as a brand name—I doubt that anyone will contact you if you do not send a résumé with your cover letter.

To be enough of a brand name to get attention with a cover letter alone, you should have a very successful business career with a major, well-known firm; or you should have been instrumental in the start-up of a very successful, smaller, but well-known firm; or you should have worked for a competitor of the firm that is seeking to fill a position.

Similarly, a person not sending a cover letter with the résumé stands less of a chance since he or she did not fully *introduce* himself. This is what we mean by protocol.

Remember that human resource personnel, recruiters, and others, such as myself, who are looking for good people, are overburdened with "known" people whom we "know" through their résumés. If you do not include your résumé, we probably will not have the time or inclination to request more information about you. It's just not being smart if you do not follow protocol.

---

[10] *Protocol* is also the term used in highly deterministic procedures, such as the way a computer program in one machine "talks to." or communicates with, a program in another machine.

SECTION 3: Waiting for the Call

- Your house is now your office—even if you have the use of an office away from home during the day. Search people and human resource managers frequently place calls at night to home numbers. (Your résumé lists your home number.)
- Get an answering machine for use when you are away. Purchase one that allows you to answer with a short message so that the beep comes quickly, avoiding long, meaningless messages.
- Keep the message short and business-like. No funny messages. No children or wives recording the message. People like to hear *your* voice. It is the first human contact they have with you. Make it work for you.
- Set the machine to pick up the call with a minimum of rings. (The toll-saving feature that is available on some machines, which gives you the option of having your machine wait for three or more rings before answering, should not be used.) This is a business courtesy.
- People know about answering machines. You do not have to explain that they are talking to an answering machine. Also, use a machine that allows you to trim your message to be as short as possible. You should not give long messages explaining that you are not available, etc., etc. You need not give instructions about a "beep." People are telephone literate. (The only benefiter from long messages is the phone company.)
- When other family members are at home and you have only one outside phone line, keep the family (spouses, too) off the line as much as you can. Better yet, put in a second line during this period, so you can have a phone dedicated to your job-seeking business.
- Keep a pencil and paper next to the phone. Do this in each location where you have an extension, including the laundry room. If other people must answer your phone, make sure they can locate the pencil and paper.
- *Do not let young children answer the phone—much less take messages.* I also advise against independent spirited teenagers who do not have any experience taking messages accurately. If you must use teenagers, train them. Practice with them, and show them how to repeat the message to the caller, even if the caller does not ask that the message be repeated.
- When anyone calls, say, for example, "(*your name*)'s residence." Say it clearly. This is good business courtesy.
  (This should all be common knowledge among management people—since they are called at home by peers and bosses during off-hours—but it is not.)

SECTION 4: Operations, or Talking with Anyone in the Potential Employer Firm—or with a Recruiter

- Read a book on salesmanship—especially if you have never been a salesperson. I suggest light, but informative books, such as *How to*

Master the Art of Selling by Tom Hopkins, a paperback published by Warner Books.[11]

- When you call anyone after you have sent your letter, leave a message with the secretary or on the voice mail system, indicating why you are calling.
- I receive many résumés daily, and some are followed up by the sender with a call—just to find out if I received the résumé. This is bothersome. Furthermore, when I return such calls, I am frequently ill-disposed toward the caller since: (1) The U.S. mail works very well; (2) If I had wanted to follow up the résumé, I would have; and (3) The résumé and cover letter should be capable of doing the job of presenting the person.

SECTION 5: Selling Yourself

- You are selling yourself—no matter what your prior position may have been. Therefore, do not be pompous or overbearing—or intimidating. Be yourself—with a bit of vigor.
- Be matter-of-fact.
- Emphasize recent positions and recent accomplishments. I suggest that you should not emphasize any job experience based on what you did more than seven years ago. *Do not dwell on* a mutual experience or mutual colleagues from a prior period (more than seven years ago). If you do not follow these suggestions, you may give the impression to the caller that you are a person who dwells in the past and has not kept up with today's business and business contacts—and is relying too much on long-past accomplishments.
- Do not be evasive if asked, "Were you fired?"—and it applies. Say yes. Many people are asked to leave in what may be termed a "firing," but many times there are circumstances that were beyond the candidate's control. Human resource people know this, and they will be open to learning the special circumstances in your case. Thus, it is better to say yes, and indicate that you wish to describe the circumstances.
- Some recruiting advisors recommend that you should not tell anyone what your present (or past) salary is. I disagree with this advice. A recruiter is interested in *you* and *wants* you if he calls you. He is trying to see if you match his requirements and the client's budget. Be open. Be clear. Be explicit. These are the essentials. State base and incentives and whether you made those incentives. They are part of your brand name campaign to differentiate you from the masses.
- Concerning references, I prefer to speak to some references prior to meeting someone in order to discuss the candidate's applicability to a position. This is to avoid the potentially wasteful process of budgeting time and travel costs—wasteful for both parties—if the references indicate that you are not right for the position.

---

[11] Tom Hopkins, *How to Master the Art of Selling* (New York: Warner Books, 1982).

Conversely if references are good, the candidate will be pursued with more vigor. Some of your references may be senior executives whom you do not wish to be bothered—except by serious potential employers. The first stage of the screening process may be too soon. All right. But you must have at least one person who knows what you did: a candid person, preferably someone who was your supervisor.

SECTION 6: A Word about Grammar

I am a stickler on this. When I hear poor grammar from a presumably well-educated person, it rubs me the wrong way. And an interviewer could have the same reaction. Therefore, brush up on your grammar.

I frequently hear about a half a dozen common faults, faults which English-speaking Americans should not commit. Some of them are not too bad, but those presented below are easily avoided.

PRONOUNS used as *objects of prepositions:*

I, he/she, we, they—are pronouns that are *subjects* in a sentence.

Me, him/her, them, us—are pronouns that are *objects* in a sentence. They may be objects of a *verb*, objects of a *preposition*, or indirect objects.

Examples

Subject	Verb	Object of the Verb
I	saw	him/her
she	saw	me
we	saw	him/her
we	saw	them
they	saw	us

Subject		Object of Preposition (to)
She	gave the ball *to*	him and me.

(*not* "he and I" nor "him and I" nor "I" nor "he and me") That is, choose the pronouns that are used as *objects.*

Words that are typically (but not always) prepositions are *to, of, from, at, on, by,* etc.

PRONOUNS used in *comparison:*

If you are going to make a comparison such as:

He is greater than
$\begin{cases} \text{he} \quad \ldots \text{or him.} \\ \text{she} \quad \ldots \text{or her.} \\ \text{we} \quad \ldots \text{or us.} \\ \text{I} \quad \ldots \text{or me.} \end{cases}$ (as many people incorrectly say

Remember that the sentence is a shortening of:

He is greater than
$\begin{cases} \text{he is.} \\ \text{she is.} \\ \text{we are.} \\ \text{I am.} \end{cases}$

"Greater than I," "greater than she," or "greater than we" may sound awkward (but correct), so end with the verb *is* or *are*, if it makes you comfortable.

UNIQUE: When something is *unique* it is "one-of-a-kind." That's it—only one. It cannot be "more unique," "very unique," etc.

Use good business communication during these difficult times because you can't afford to make the wrong impression by making errors.

SECTION 7: Where to Look for a Job

In looking for a job, perhaps the most important decision you will make is *where* you will be looking for one. The tables presented in Part II can help calibrate yourself and define your geographic limits so that you will not waste time and money foolishly.

Location will condition how your potential employer may consider you. He will consider costs and may wonder whether you will actually show up on the day you promised you would, or whether you will leave the firm in a few months to return to where you lived before joining his firm.

For example, he will have in the back of his mind whether you are a "high-cost-to-move person" and, if so, why would he want to move you? That is, are you a strong enough brand name for the employer to undertake a new major expense? He may be concerned that if your spouse is presently employed, he or she may decide at the last moment not to move, since it may be unclear what his/her job may be in the new location. Or your spouse may decide at the last moment that he or she does not want to uproot the family. Or your potential employer may anticipate that you may have a housing problem due to the difference in the cost of housing and the accompanying need for a larger down payment than you can afford, even by selling your present home. This is especially true if your present area's housing market is in a depressed condition.

The message in all of this is that it is highly unlikely you will get a job outside your geographic area unless you possess some brand name features such as coming from a highly successful firm (or working for a competitor) or working in a specialty that is in great demand, or, in the case of recent graduates, having attended excellent schools. As a rule, do not bother looking in a place that is far from where you are unless it happens to be in a booming, expansive area.

I have personally observed how often people reply to ads when there is really no chance to be called for an interview. From time to time, I have assisted firms in searches they conducted to fill mid-level positions. I assisted them by placing ads in major local newspapers and in the *Wall Street Journal* and then helped the client evaluate the résumés that the ads attracted. The ads always specified the city where the candidates would be working. These were not special positions. They did not call for special requirements. They covered such areas as human resources, general sales, administration, finance, etc. When the replies came, I observed that more than half were from people living out of the state, many in states at least 1,500 miles from the job site. My client firm was concerned about costs—salary, moving, potential delays, etc. Most firms are. In most cases, we looked at the postmark and did not even open the envelopes of the long-distance letters, let alone review the prospects.

Geographic Areas

During the past 10 years, geographic areas of growth have been Greater Boston, the Research Triangle in North Carolina, Austin and Dallas in Texas, Atlanta, and the phenomenal Silicon Valley. These areas have also developed a broad base of jobs to support the key industries of the locale: jobs in both service and industrial firms, in the areas of installation and maintenance firms, printing and "stuffing" of circuit boards, and delivery services. There are hundreds of these growing firms, both large and small, making up what economists call "the infrastructure." And, moreover, this infrastructure is not tied to one industry, as is the case for the petrochemical industry centered in Houston.

In my personal examination of these areas, in particular, the Silicon Valley of Northern California and the Boston area, I have tried to understand why they have grown as much as they have. What are the ingredients that made these areas more successful and dynamic than others? And how were they able to accomplish this in a steady way and provide benefits to all levels of people in the economic ladder?

If recreational facilities and cultural amenities were a deciding factor, New York would certainly be on the same level as Boston and the Silicon Valley. If climate were the key, North Carolina and Dallas might rank with California, and Boston would be in the second rank. The answer goes beyond this, beyond even the incentives any state can provide for the growth of industry. Based on my own observations, I believe that the key to high growth is the development of *entrepreneurial technology*.

The basic necessity, of course, is the presence of schools that are strong in engineering technology and business. In the Silicon Valley, Stanford has an excellent M.B.A. program, the Sloan program for executives, and strong technology programs in computer science, chemistry, biology, engineering, etc. In the Boston area, there is M.I.T., with an equally broad-based technology program and the Sloan School for technology-oriented M.B.A.s, as well as Harvard with its renowned business school. Other areas have fine schools as well: New York University and Columbia in New York; the University of Texas at Austin; the Golden Triangle of the University of North Carolina; North Carolina State; and Duke. Twenty years ago, when computers, electronics, and bioengineering were still in their infancy, a combination of good science and good business programs was enough. Now it is necessary to have a highly developed technology program operating within a business-oriented environment. That is what sets Boston and the Silicon Valley apart from other growth areas.

To understand this point further, it is helpful to look at the nature of the faculty at different schools, even within the same area.

The Faculty

It is not enough just to have a strong engineering school to start new businesses. The engineering or technology school must also have people on its faculty who have entrepreneurial mentalities. From what I have seen, the graduates of Harvard's M.B.A. program usually think of becoming general managers and CEOs in large firms, whereas the graduates of M.I.T. are more likely to ask themselves, "What industry shall I start?" That is the business start-up syndrome that you find at M.I.T. and Stanford—something which may not be as strong in most other technology schools.

Given the fertile growth environment, the professors frequently have consulting assignments from firms in the area, both for business and for technology problems. They develop and maintain an entrepreneurial attitude, since they are frequently participating in the early stages of the firms' development. They may receive pay, a role on the board, and equity.

Since the faculty may have more assignments than they can handle, they may pass some of their work—for pay—to their graduate students. Thus, the graduate students, in an early stage in their professional career, are exposed to business and technical problems as seen by their mentors, the professor-consultants. They learn to see a problem as top-management sees it.

The student gets to know the key problem areas: product planning, product strategy, product architecture, business planning, resource allocation, market planning, etc. What an education—to learn right at the start what business is all about and, more importantly, to be able to exercise and experience your own business potential at an early age.

There is another way larger firms in these areas react to the entrepreneurial environment. In order to keep their people from joining new start-up ventures, they are obliged to pay them well, a factor that makes it easier to attract the better candidates.

The Potential in the High-Growth Area

The significance of this to people in the job search, especially when they are in their 30s and 40s is that they should look at the entrepreneurial, business and technology regions as growth areas that will support a wide variety of jobs and businesses—supporting people even when they are not well versed in the local technologies.

While the cost of living in these areas is sometimes higher than in other areas, these areas always have the opportunity for people to seek present and future jobs, and they provide the possibility of learning a new trade or profession.

For those people who have not visited any of these high-growth areas, I suggest that they contact friends and former colleagues now living in these regions, as well as various departments of commerce of the region. I also suggest your picking up the region's local newspapers to get a sense of the growth and the opportunities that are available.

Think of taking a trip or spending a vacation there to see what the areas offer and to get a feel of what the area is like. You may see a dynamism and an environment opportunity that may astound you.

PART VII

MY FINAL REMARKS—SOME HOMILIES

Do not have preconceived ideas about who may want to hire you. Be open about where you send your résumé—but be reasonable.

If you have been with a firm for most of your career (more than 15 years, let us say), spend as many months as you can (up to at least three) recalibrating yourself. Do not go looking for a job immediately. Talk to people in your industry. Learn what has been going on outside your firm. Find out the reality of your expectations, what you can bring to bear in the market, and how to position and package yourself.

In any job search, you will be turned down for something you really set your sights on. Keep in mind that Babe Ruth struck out more than one thousand times. He is remembered for hitting 741 home runs.

All you need is ONE successful interview and job offer. Don't worry about the GNP, a recession, the high unemployment rate, etc. You are a unique person, not a statistic.

Remember, YOU make your day. When you wake up in the morning and plan to devote another day to your job search, start with a positive and cheerful attitude—and keep it up. No one is sending you to jail; the bank is not foreclosing on your mortgage; American Express will wait a few more days; your family loves you; your health is fine. You *will* find a job if you work at it. So what are you worrying about?